Sixty Years
of Cuttin' the Cheese

For my neighbors Jim + Eileen.

Sixty Years of Cuttin' the Cheese

Joel Sherburne and Calef's Famous Country Store

Rebecca Rule 9-23-2017

By Rebecca Rule

Published by
Peter E. Randall Publisher
Portsmouth, NH
2017

ISBN13: 9781937721473
Library of Congress Control no.: 2017944792

Published by
Peter E. Randall Publisher
5 Greenleaf Woods Drive, Suite #102
Portsmouth, NH 03801
www.perpublisher.com

Visit the store:
Calef's Country Store
606 Franklin Pierce Highway
Barrington, NH 03825
http://www.calefs.com

Contact the author:
Rebecca Rule
178 Mountain Avenue
Northwood, NH 03261
http://www.rebeccarulenh.com/

Acknowledgments

Thanks to all the folks who work at Calef's who welcomed me on my frequent visits during the interview and research process and never made me feel like I was underfoot, even though I probably was. Thanks to Melanie Giehl, Calef's manager, who made the connections and kept the communication going from beginning to end.

To the folks who attended the gab fest to share stories about Calef's and Joel, your contributions brought a lot of color to this book and are much appreciated—thanks Dr. Jo Laird, Billy McGowan, the Waterhouses—Dan, Les, and Barbara—John Maiorino, David Ranson, Mary Ann and David Gatchell, Helen Musler; and those whose names I've left out—please forgive me; there was a lot of coming and going that afternoon.

Alberta Calef St. Cyr's unique perspective, candor, good humor were much appreciated.

Michael Sterling, photographer, volunteered to come out to Calef's and take some special photographs just for this book. That was a fun session!

Facebook friends, thanks for sharing your stories of your favorite country stores.

Carolyn Handy, the last editor at the *Tri-Town Transcript*, stood in the pouring rain and hauled many large boxes out of a storage unit to help locate a lot of the photographs that add so much to this book. Thanks Carolyn—you went above and beyond! Thanks to John Rule, also, for hauling boxes in the rain.

Thanks to the gang at Peter E. Randall Publisher for your knowledge, your efficiency, your great ideas, your encouragement, and hard work. Well done!

Greg Bolton: You made this book happen with your vision and unwavering support.

And Joel, my friend—what can I say? This is your train. I just came along for the ride.

Joel Sherburne and Rebecca Rule pose behind the cheese counter. Cheese makes us happy.

Contents

Smoky Cheese Chowder Recipe

Ingredients

- 1 10-oz. pkg. frozen whole kernel corn
- ½ cup chopped onion
- ½ cup water
- 1 tsp. instant chicken bouillon granules
- ¼ tsp. pepper
- 2 ½ cups milk
- 3 Tbsp. all-purpose flour
- 4 oz. grated Calef's Smoked Cheddar
- 1 Tbsp. diced pimento, drained

Directions

In a saucepan combine corn, onion, water, bouillon, & pepper. Bring to a boil, reduce heat. Cover & simmer about 4 minutes or until corn is tender. Do not drain. Stir together milk & flour; then stir into corn mixture until thickened & bubbly. Stir in pimento & cheese until cheese melts & serve hot. Serves four.

Introduction

In 2011 when my business partner and I began looking for an opportunity to call our own, we came upon the listing for Calef's Country Store in Barrington, NH. His family, being from northern Massachusetts and frequent travelers of RT 125, had been to Calef's many times. In spite of being a NH native I had not, but I made a clandestine visit and quickly became intrigued. This opportunity had many of the necessary business requirements that we were looking for, but also had one more important thing, a compelling story. It is a rare combination to acquire an ongoing viable business and an important piece of NH history simultaneously.

Calef's owner Greg Bolton at the table in the middle of the store where folks gather to talk or have a bite to eat.

I had heard about the staff and more importantly Joel from Lindy Horton, the previous owner, during the sales process. Little did I know what I was in for. I first met Joel during the final building inspection; we needed to visit the store during operating hours so Lindy told the staff she was having an insurance inspection. The sale was still not public knowledge. As four of us filed through the back door Joel nodded to each of us, "Hallo, hallo, hallo, hallo…insurance, huh?" As they say, that was the start of an incredible relationship. Joel and the entire staff welcomed us into their world in spite of the fact that we didn't have a clue. We are fortunate to have such a dedicated caring staff.

It became apparent from the start that our role was far more important than typical business owners; we had become stewards of Calef's. Maintaining the integrity of the business is the driving force. Clearly there are things about the store over which we have little or no say. Our staff and more importantly our customers are quite vocal if we head down the wrong path. There continues to be a tremendous sense of pride about Calef's in the community and we now see our role much differently. Occasionally I will hear the words, "Well, it is your store," in response to an idea that I might float. I have learned that this

A youngster practices math in the candy corner. So many choices!

is really code for "That's a dumb idea." One example is how we sell our famous penny candy. Each item is priced by the piece. I had the stroke of genius to start selling it by the pound. Every other store does this, so why didn't we? So much faster, so much easier for the cashiers, people will spend more, more efficient, the list of good reasons goes on. What I failed to consider is that many families use our penny candy counter as a math lesson for their children. "Sally, you have $2.00 to spend" and Sally needs to make choices and do the math so that her bag totals $2.00. That seems like the country store way to me and so that is what we continue to do.

I consider myself fortunate to have gotten to know Joel and to have had the opportunity to work with him over these past four years. He is an exemplary person who puts others before himself, as you will learn as you read his story. His dedication to Calef's has been unwavering, I suspect, for his entire adult life. He is a wealth of knowledge and opinion when it comes to the store. I can only imagine the countless number of high school, college, and adult workers he has seen come and go from Calef's, yet he welcomes each new employee with open arms and an open heart. He teaches them the same tasks that he has taught countless others who have moved on and he tells the same jokes and stories that have been part of his repertoire for generations. Customers always ask after him if he is not in the store when they visit. Many are former employees who have moved on with their lives but come back to pay Joel a visit and get some Snappy Old Cheese. Others are people who have been regular customers since their childhood, and Joel is as much a part of their Calef's memory as the wood stove or the pickle barrel. To say that Joel is an institution is to sell him a bit short. He has chosen a simple life in his hometown that truly makes him happy every day. How many of us can say that? Up until recently Joel worked seven days a week. He has since cut back to five, but it is a common for him to stop in on his days off and be sure we are all set. If he sees something amiss he will don his trademark white apron and get us caught up. That is who he is!

Country stores are not unique to New England, but there seem to be more here than in most other parts of the country. Some are gone, some survive, and some thrive. We are among the fortunate: Calef's thrives. This can be attributed to several factors, some illustrated above. However, the single most important factor is our location. We are in a large, iconic white colonial building at the junction of two major roads in rural NH. Many other country stores have fallen victim to the highway bypass, which has taken all their traffic and rerouted it around the town center. Out of sight, out of mind; as they say: location, location, location. Without the traffic passing our doors every day, we could have the best of everything and too few customers. Our location allows us to have a unique blend of local and tourist traffic visiting our store every day. Given our great traffic count and two distinct customer bases, our job to appeal to both is not without challenges. The tourist traffic likes the feeling they are in a local store, but the local trade is not at all interested in visiting a tourist trap. Our product mix, customer service and

The old building still looks good—she's been well cared for over the years by the Calef family as well as the Hortons and now Greg Bolton and company.

staff help bridge the two. Our country deli has been instrumental in keeping a strong local following.

Many of my friends and colleagues who have known me in other vocations say that I am finally doing what I was meant to do, running a country store. I can wear jeans and flannel to work and that is what's expected. We have no hard, fast rules other than take care of the customer. If we try something and it doesn't work, then we try something else. We don't have thick manuals full of policies, rules, and procedures. Instead we have good, smart, hard-working people who act in the best interests of the store. What more could any business owner ask for?

Greg Bolton
March 2017

Cheese Balls

Cream 1 cup (about ¼ pound) of grated Calef's Aged Cheddar with ½ cup butter or margarine.

Mix in 1 cup flour, ½ teaspoon Tabasco sauce, and 1 cup of Rice Krispies©.

Shape into marble-sized balls and ungreased baking sheet at 350°F for 10–12 minutes or until lightly browned.

Store the Cheese Balls in a closed container in your refrigerator.

Prologue

How This Book Came to Be

Melanie Giehl shot me an email. I knew her from Calef's Country Store in Barrington, New Hampshire—just fifteen minutes from my house—where I sometimes told stories, signed books, and bought gifts. She and Greg Bolton, the owner, had an idea for a book—the story of Calef's Country Store told through the eyes and memory of long-time employee, Joel Sherburne. The book would celebrate Joel's sixty years of

Joel, Greg, and Cindy Jupp-Jones from WMUR during the filming of a segment for the television program *New Hampshire Chronicle*.

working at Calef's and the store's 150th anniversary. It would also celebrate all old-fashioned general stores, symbols of small-town America.

I signed on to the project in a heartbeat. And, so—thankfully and without too much arm twisting—did Joel. Throughout the spring of 2016, we met weekly at a round table in the center of the store next to the wood stove, in front of the shelves (yes, shelves) of pepper jellies and within sniffing distance of the hot coffee. I brought questions, but often didn't have to ask any. Joel came well prepared with stories he'd come up with during the week. He'd say, "Today I want to talk about…." And off we'd go.

We were frequently interrupted by customers passing through. "Hey, Joel!" A quick hello, a little chat, maybe a hug. Some were star struck—"We were hoping to see you, Joel, and there you sit!" One couple from Moultonborough drove more than fifty miles on the off chance of catching Joel in action. They were not disappointed. They'd seen him on the television show *Chronicle*. "Shocking, wasn't it?" Joel said. "They got my good side. I told them, 'You better get my good side or don't put it in.'"

Seems like Joel is as much of a draw as the heaping barrel of old-fashioned gingersnaps. Many were friends. "My God," Joel would say, "I haven't seen you in a long time. How you doing?" Some passed through most every day. Joel would call out a name: "Cleve!" Then fill me in, "Cleve's getting his coffee before he heads ovah to the hardware stoah. Yuh, he's working over theyah now." (Cleve and Lindy Horton owned the store after the Calef's and before Greg Bolton.)

The interruptions were part of the fun—part of the burlap of life at Calef's Country Store. And believe me, it is lively. Music played. Clerks buzzed through. Shelves were continually restocked. Pile 'em high, watch 'em fly. That's the motto of the general store. If there's a lot of something, it must be good, like those gingersnaps.

Customers studied the abundance of merchandise and filled their baskets. Real wicker baskets—none of those plastic ones like you see at BiggieMart. Some customers just filled a cup with coffee and drank it slowly. No hurries, no worries. The wall phone rang regularly, loudly—just couple rings before an invisible somebody picked up. If someone walked through the door and shouted a cheery, "Hello, Calef's people," you could be sure she was a local.

After many weeks of one-on-one talks, a group of Joel's friends and colleagues gathered at that same table for a walk down memory aisle. Mel organized it. We had no idea who would show up at 4:00 on a Wednesday afternoon. If anybody. Greg provided snacks, including cheese. Of course there would be cheese. It's not Calef's without the cheese.

Well, they came. Some stayed two hours, some just a few minutes. We had to bring out extra chairs. Some told their favorite stories of Joel and Calef's. Some told stories completely unrelated to Joel and Calef's but none-the-less entertaining. Others just listened and enjoyed the snacks and the company.

Much of what you'll read in these pages comes from my many talks with Joel and from that cheesy gab session. We covered a lot of territory. Alberta Calef St. Cyr, the last of the family to own the store, met with me at her home. We had a good talk about family history, Joel as a teenager, her husband Roger, and the hard decision after Roger's untimely death to let the store go out of the family.

Additional information comes from books, articles, the Internet, and so-forth—all listed in the back. But for starters, here it is—the story of Joel Sherburne and Calef's Famous Country Store. As Joel would say, I hope it floats your boat. That's what we called a Joelism. Watch for them, we've sprinkled them around like red pepper on a calf's nose.

We've also included Calef's best cheese recipes—some tucked into the chapters themselves where appropriate. We've also collected the whole load of recipes at the end for easy reference. You're welcome.

Happy cooking. Happy eating. And happy reading.

Rebecca Rule
March 2017

Cheese Coins

Cream 2 cups (about ½ pound) grated Calef's Aged Cheddar with ½ cup margarine or butter. Add 1 and ½ cups flour.

Mix in your choice of one of the following: 1 Tablespoon chives, ½ teaspoon onion powder, ½ teaspoon cayenne pepper, or ½ teaspoon Tabasco sauce.

Roll dough into a 2-inch diameter log, wrap in cellophane or wax paper and refrigerate for at least 2 hours. You may also freeze these logs for baking at a later date.

After refrigeration, slice very thin (like coins) and bake on an ungreased cookie sheet at 350°F for 15 minutes or until lightly browned.

≋ Chapter 1 ≋

An Institution Within an Institution

For a hundred and fifty years, the general store at the intersection of routes 9 and 125 in Barrington, New Hampshire (population almost 9,000), has been called by the one name, Calef's Country Store. For all but the last few years, it was owned and run by one family, the Calefs. It is an institution.

Joel Sherburne, Calef's star employee for sixty years and counting, goes by many names. He is also an institution.

I made the mistake of saying, "Why Joel, you are Mr. Calef's!"

"No," he shot back, "I'm Mr. Sherburne." Pronounced, "Mistah Shubun." With just the hint of two *r*'s in his last name and no hidden *r*'s at all, not even a breath of one, in the *Mister*.

Joel's accent and delivery are remarkable. His deliberate cadence and crisp enunciation remind many of how their grandparents or great-grandparents spoke, harkening to earlier times and a more rural and insulated New Hampshire. Actually, if you listen to WOKQ, the country radio station out of Dover, you've

Snappy old cheese in a firkin. You can even buy the little cast iron mouse, purely decorative.

1

probably heard him in radio ads telling listeners about Calef's and its signature Snappy Old Cheese. Yup, he's a media sensation. "We'll bring you back to the 60s," he intones, "the 1860s, that is."

"I guess it may be the accent," Joel says about why the ads are so popular. "A lot of people think I do this on purpose. But I don't. It's just natural. I'd go down to the station and record it. Right down to WOKQ. They have a big studio. Oh my God, state of the aht. I'd go in and they'd record me. They thought it was terrific! I liked to do it. It really brought people in here. They'd say, I heard you on the radio or I seen you on the television."

For Joel, it is a compliment and a bit of a trial that he's recognized pretty much everywhere he goes, not so much by his face as his voice. "I can't go anywhere with my voice but they'll say to me, 'I've heard you somewhere. Now let me think.' Even Market Basket or anything. I'll say, 'Well have you heard of Calef's Country Stoah.' They'll say, 'That's it!'"

I have a New Hampshire accent, too. And proud of it. Many of us in the Granite State do. We border Maine, Massachusetts, Vermont,

Among Joel's many talents—stand-up comedy. Here he is as Country Joel, Comedian.

and Quebec, so we share elements of those four distinctive dialects, depending on what part of the state we hail from. For me the accent comes and goes, strong or subdued, according to the situation. (I delude myself into thinking I can control it.) But Joel's accent is pure and consistent. He sprinkles his *r*'s in surprising places, but generally represses them. His *a*'s are broad, more *uh* than *ah*. He often draws a single syllable into two, savoring each one. Case-in-point, the word store, sto-ah. Or sure, pronounced sho-ah. Or his first name, Jo-el.

Some of his other titles make him shake his head. When I list them, he says, "I've been called worse." Here are a few:

- President of the Barrington Historical Society
- Founder of the Barrington Ambulance Service
- EMT of the Year
- Country Joel, Comedian
- Ambassador and Announcer for the Rochester Fair
- Founder of and Ambassador for NH Lighthouse Week (third week of June)
- Notary and Justice of the Peace
- Member in Good Standing of Circus Fans of America
- Barrington Citizen of the Year
- The Mayor of Barrington
- Barrington Treasure
- The Voice of Calef's
- And, of course, The Cheese Man

Joelism —"Makes your livah quivvah." As in: "Going to the circus and gettin' to stand in the ring with the ringmaster, so excitin', made my livah quivvah."

He makes an impression—tall, lanky, full head of stiff gray hair, intense blue eyes that catch you in their high-beams and don't let go. Engaged in conversation, Joel stays pretty much stone faced, in the Yankee tradition, unless and until when truly amused he breaks into a face-splitting grin and says something like, "That's a good one!" Sometimes he literally slaps his knee.

"Becky," he says, "you ah funny!"

"Jo-el," I say, "so ah you!"

On the job, he's always in uniform—a white butcher's apron adorned with a pin that reads "Big" with a picture of a wedge of cheese underneath. A friend spotted the pin at a shop in Ogunquit and couldn't resist. Joel's been sporting it ever since. Yup, he's the Big Cheese.

3

He made a big impression on John Maiorino the first time they met at a Chamber of Commerce mixer years ago. John's from away—far away: Connecticut. He'd just bought the Nippo Lake Golf Club, the venue for the mixer. He describes the meeting with a fully realized impression of Joel's accent and inflections, honed over time and many tellings.

At the meet and greet, each attendee received the name tag of another person to seek out and get to know though a series of pre-scribed questions. "So I get Joel Sherburne," John says. "I track him down. I introduce myself. Of course, I gotta ask him some questions."

Doing his Joel impression, John sends his voice up and down on a musical scale. The high notes are in bold.

"So Joel, where do you work?"

"Joel says, '**Whay**uh do I **work**? I work at **Cay**lef's Country **Sto**ah.'"

John pressed on. "I gotta ask him the other questions. So I say, 'That's really good, Joel, how long you been working there?'

Joel says, "How **long** have I been **work**in' they-uh? For as long as I can **ruh-mem-buh**."

The next question (perhaps only in my imagination) may have been: "What do you do at Calef's Country Store?"

Joel: "What do I **do** at **Cay**lef's Country **Sto**ah? I cut **cheese**."

And so forth.

John says, "After I get this information, we all get together and I have to tell everybody what he said. It got quite a round of applause. They liked Joel's answers."

Course they did, John. Everybody in Barrington (pretty much) knows Joel Sherburne. Gosh, pretty much anywhere in the state, if I drop his name, somebody in the crowd will know him or know of him. Most everybody who knows him or of him knows where he works. And as for the cheese, well, Calef's Snappy Old Cheese is known and admired and consumed statewide, countrywide—worldwide, truth be told.

Most everybody knows Joel and his connection with Calef's, except John Maiorino all those years ago. John says, "I'm a flatlander. What do you want from me?"

Twenty years later, John still tells the story. And others tell the story of John telling the story of his first meeting with Joel Sherburne. It is the stuffing of legend.

As Told by Joel

The Pregnant Turkey

We sold native turkeys and had to draw 'em here. The turkeys would come in from different farms. We had a tendon puller out back on the wall. One turkey farmer lived right in Madbury. He showed me a lot in drawing turkeys, and I don't mean on paper and with a pen. I mean cleaning 'em out and getting 'em ready.

That was excitin'.

Way back then we had quite a few orders that we had to fill.

We always started with you-know-what cut. The rectum cut. That's how you done it. Had to be careful you don't puncture anything. They were already plucked when we got 'em. Take 'em to the sink and flush 'em. We flushed 'em right out. Save the heart, the liver, the gizzard. A lot of 'em didn't want to do it. But I didn't mind.

Never got a complaint from the turkey.

Harlan knew a doctor in Rochester that always got a turkey here. You know these Cornish hens, about a pound and a half, two pounds. Well, Harlan took a Cornish hen and put it in the turkey. And when the doctor come, course he paid for the turkey, and it was all in a plastic bag and everything. When he got home and got ready to fix the turkey, he found this Cornish hen inside the turkey.

He called right up the store. He said, "I want to speak to Harlan." So they put Harlan on. He said, "Harlan, when I got here and got that turkey out to fix it to put it in the oven, there was somethin' in it."

"Well, yes," Harlan said. "Your turkey had a baby."

I guess the doctor said, "Oh my God." Something like that.

Oh it went over good.

Mary Ann Gatchell, an old friend of both Joel and Calef's, says, "You just want to come in and talk to Joel. He's up 99% of the time."

Dr. Jo Laird, among Calef's most faithful customers, says, "I've known him for thirty-five years. He hasn't changed a lot as far as I can tell."

Joel adds a dose of reality, "Very seldom do I get upset but when I do you'd remember it. It's normal."

Mary Ann adds, "He's the same lovable person he was when we met him in '75." Nineteen seventy-five that is.

"I've always loved Barrington," Joel says. "I still do."

I think it's safe to say, Barrington loves him back.

≋ Chapter 2 ≋

Still Standing
After All These Years

The story of Calef's and Joel is the story of countless dedicated employees and country stores in New England and across the country. One in every town, pretty much—had to be. These modest buildings, centrally located, provided a place to buy staples and commune with neighbors. Most, sadly, have been replaced by chain convenience stores, gas stations, and big-ass box stores. I blame the proliferation of cars and all the smooth roads we've built to drive them on.

These days, people spend as much time out of town as in. Our roots don't reach as deeply into the soil of home as they used to. We're not as connected to place and neighbors, not as dependent on each other. Independence? That's a good thing. Feel free to move about the county, the state, the country, the world. Follow opportunity. But with that independence our sense of place-based community suffers. Is the place where we sleep truly our town, or just a town in which we happen to live for the time being? The family that settles a place and stays through five or seven generations—that's rare. The Calefs are such a family. As are the Sherburnes. Every small town claims a few of these anchor families—anchors in the sense of holding steady, with sturdy connections. These anchor families provide a town with a strong sense of identity and continuity.

Used to be the country store stood at the center of these tight-knit, deeply rooted communities. It carried a little bit of everything. It was patronized by everybody in town because they had few other shopping choices. These were the days when Amazon was a river in South America and Target was a bullseye for practicing your aim. These were the days when a trip out of town (or even to the other side of town) constituted an event, rare and carefully planned. The country store thrived in an era of sticking close to home and shopping locally out of necessity and practicality. For the most part that era has passed. And many of these stores have closed or been transformed into gift shops, cafes, offices, apartments, even furniture stores for country-style living.

Joelism —"Goin' down to the city." As in: "My gout's acting up. Gotta go down to the city to see if the doc can cure what ails me."

Goin' down to the city describes an expedition to any place with a population bigger than Barrington's, for example Dover, Rochester, Portsmouth, Concord, Manchester, or Exeter.

But Calef's thrives, somewhat transformed but not so changed that it doesn't retain its country store ambiance. It thrives on cheese, soup, sandwiches, dried beans, hot sauces, trademark mugs, sundries, souvenirs, books (like this one), cheerful service, customer loyalty, and a healthy dose of nostalgia.

Joel says, "We never had beer here for a long while. Eventually they kind of give in and said 'I guess we got to do it.' Because so many come in and asked for it. Now we've got all kinds." From craft brews like Out Haus Ales (brewed next door in Northwood) to not-so-crafty Budweiser, Calef's rolls with the times. Got to.

Many of the products in the store today carry the Calef's label and most of them are New England-made. If an item carries the Calef's name it must be of high quality. There's 150 years of reputation to uphold. In bygone days, their specialty was whatever anybody needed to cook, clean, spruce up, repair, feed the livestock, or stay warm come winter. Today, a vigorous on-line business supplements and, at times, even surpasses in-store sales. Thanks to the Internet, Calef's brand products ship all over this country and to many other countries as well.

"If we ain't got it, you don't need it." That was the motto of all country stores worth their rock salt. Soup to nuts doesn't begin to cover it—more like chicken feed to monkey wrenches, crackers to work boots, tuna fish to tires. How about: apples to zippers?

A few things have changed dramatically. The use of computers, for example, to support on-line sales and keep track of inventory, orders, payroll. When you check out, the computer calculates your tab. Gone are the old-fashioned cash registers, bells ringing, ka-ching. Even longer gone are the hand-penciled bills of sale. The beans in the deli still cook slow, but the computer works fast. "Chalk it up," Joel says. You won't find him pushing buttons at the checkout. Most any other job, sure. But computers, no thanks.

Is that a jar of pickled limes at lower right? Some love 'em. Others not so much.

Still, much at Calef's has stayed the same. Essentials like the gin-gersnap cookies with extra snap—they're bitey! And not-so-essentials like pickled limes, an old-time favorite. Or were they?

They're supposed to be good for your stomach. "If you can get 'em down there," Joel says. "I never could. Most horrible tasting thing I think I ever had. But we sell a lot of 'em."

One customer from North Carolina had a standing order for two dozen pickled limes every two months. "She loved 'em," Joel says. "But a lot of 'em come in here and they'll say, 'I never heard of a pickled lime. What is it?' I say, 'It's a lime—pickled.'"

Calef's was and is (far as I know) the only place in Barrington you can buy pickled limes. There's a jar of them on the deli counter—look-ing delectable. Sort of.

The pickling is done on site in barrels. Cucumber pickles are, of course, a favorite.

"Dill is great," Joel says, "but sow-ah gives you puck-uh pow-uh.

As Told by Joel
(with a twinkle in both his eyes)

You know these young girls would come in with those mini-skirts on and they'd say, "Where's the biggest pickle?" And I'd say, "Near the bottom of the barrel."

So you can imagine what happened.

Yass.

Just dive right in.

Ain't that a good line?

Joelism —"Ass ova tea kettle." As in: Ahthuh was loadin' his pick-up, slipped on patch of ice and went ass over tea kettle. I said, "Ahthuh, you hurt yourself?"

Ahthuh says, "Didn't do me any good."

As tastes changed so did the offerings—especially in the food line. Salted herring, for example: "We used to sell a lot of it," Joel says. "I didn't care for it. I'm not too keen on chewing up bones."

At one time, whole salt cod fish hung from hooks in the meat department. "We'd hack a slab off," Joel says, "weigh it up. It went very good with bread-and-milk or cracker-and-milk. Some would buy a slab and say to me, 'I'm going home tonight and I'm going to have some cracker milk and some of this cod fish.' It was all cooked. Oh yes."

You don't hear too much about salt cod any more, but for many years it was a New England favorite. Before refrigeration, salting was the go-to method for preserving the fish that were so abundant in New England's coastal waters. Fishermen in the 1600s (when the

The old wooden pickle barrel. Dill is great, but sow-ah gives you puck-uh pow-uh.

11

Puritans were boating over from England) declared: "We came for cod, not for God."

Joel says: "After the cod hung around awhile, then they come out with wooden boxes. They packed the cod in those little wooden boxes. Now you see those boxes for sale in the antique shops." Where can you find a nice salted cod these days? Not at Calef's. Not anymore.

Pickled pigs feet were another popular item. A customer who asked for a couple of pig feet would get Joel's standard response: "Do you want left or right?"

"What's the difference?"

"The right one is a little more tenduh."

Joel says, "No truth to it atall," in the Yankee tradition of never letting the truth stand in the way of a good story.

"We had the hocks too," he says. "This was way back. They come in about a two-and-a-half-gallon jug. My grandmother loved 'em. And she loved the smoked herring. She couldn't help it!"

Whatever a person wanted in the meat line, Calef's carried it. Beef liver, pork liver, calves liver, even head cheese, which is a jelly of beef and

Calef's parade entry, 1922. A country store loves its community and the community loves it back.

pork, traditionally made of flesh from the head—minus ears, brain, and eyeballs. Joel says, "I didn't especially rave for head cheese but it was ok. It was different."

Tripe, another old-time favorite, can still be found on the menus at local diners—true diners that also serve corned chowder and fried liver with onions. Tripe, if you don't know, is the lining of a cow's stomach. Joel says, "Ed Douglas. He was funny. A riot to work with. He was even funny to look at, little shot guy, kinda chunky. These young girls would come in and they'd think tripe was fish. He'd never tell them the difference. He said, 'If they think that's what it is, let 'em think it.'"

Clearly the characters who work at a country store and the characters who patronize it are part of the charm. Joel has always enjoyed the work. But he also enjoys the characters, especially the ones who made him laugh. Every day. Many folks associated with Calef's say that Joel makes them laugh. Every day. That's part of his charm.

Joel's friend and former boss, Alberta Calef St. Cyr says: "He's such a jokester. Oh dear. But I must say, the store was a happy place. It always seemed like a happy place. People go to Calef's because of Joel. From the time that he was probably twenty years old he was part of Calef's store. Very much so. Our help they stayed forever. We didn't have a big turnover. You knew them all your life."

As Told by Joel

Ed Douglas and the Oyster Shells

Ed lived down at Dover Point with his wife, Liz. She says, "Now Douglas, when you go to work tomorrow morning, you take them bag of oyster shells and throw 'em out the window when you get to the big bridge."

He said, "All right, deah, I will."

So the next morning, he grabbed his lunch, grabbed the bag of oyster shells, and when he got to the bridge he put the window down and tossed the bag into the river. He says, "The minute I threw

13

that bag out, I had a funny feeling. It was my lunch." He says, "I still got them oyster shells. Am I gonna get it tonight when she gets home!"

Next day, somebody saw a thermos floating in the river. They grabbed it. They said, "That looks like Ed Douglas' thermos." So he got it back.

He had a hearing aid, and he'd get home and shut it right off. Every so often, he'd say, "Yes, deah."

One night he shouldn'ta said it. She figured out he was shutting it off and not paying no attention to her. Yeah, she kinda laid into him.

I've never been married.

That's why I'm so happy and get along with everybody.

Joelism —"Flat as a fritter." As in: "It was some icy. And there Ahthuh lay, spread-eagled in the doah yahd and flat as a fritter."

After horseless carriages became popular and started running the roads, Calef's installed pumps to gas 'em up. Joel took his turn pumping gas. He did a little bit of everything, mastered pretty much all the jobs there were to master. And he passed his knowledge on to the new hires. Still does.

"We had two pumps," he says, "one going and one coming. It was excitin'."

Pumping gas was not his favorite job. "For one thing, breathing the fumes will kill your brain cells," I said.

Joel said: "I can't afford to lose too many more."

One day Joel had gas duty. He happened to be busy out back when a customer pulled up to the pumps. One of the young clerks, thinking quick, skipped out to do the pumping.

Joelism —"Gotta wet down the daisies." As in: Joel wasn't available to pump the gas. He'd excused himself. "Gotta go," he said. "Gotta wet down the daisies."

It was one of these new-fangled Volkswagens, Joel said, and the clerk didn't know too much about the design, you know, where the engine was and so forth. The clerk started pumping the gas where the oil was supposed to go.

Joel said, "I guess somebody come along and hollered 'What are you doing?' The clerk said, 'Well, I'm putting gas in this car.' Well, the fella said, 'You got the wrong hole, buddy.'"

Calef's no longer sells gas. Joel recalls they had to stop when the state stepped in—environmental regulations. "Harlan kinda fought it," Joel says. "He talked to the state. He thought he had a few pulls, a few strings, but the gas went. Didn't work. Times change." The pumps were removed when Alberta decided to sell the store. Prospective owners wanted them gone. And they went.

A fill-up of gas, a slab of salted cod, a pound of dried beans, a pair of boots, an oil lamp, or a sack of grain, Calef's had it all. And if, by

The old gas pumps back in the day. They got 'em comin' and goin'.

some rare chance, somebody wanted something the store didn't stock, that item could and would be special ordered. Les Waterhouse worked at Calef's as a young man, before Joel was born.

"I didn't know anything happened around here before Joel was born," I said to Les. He assured me there was, indeed, life before Joel— it's just that most people don't remember that far back. Les does. Like Joel, he started working at the store in high school. Generations of Barrington kids did. And still do.

Les says: "After we got electricity, my father wanted a radio. We got the house wired. My father said, 'I gotta have a radio.' So he told Clarence Calef. Clarence said, 'I can get you just what you want.' And he did. A Zenith. A big one, bright thing, a beautiful piece of furniture. A big dial on the front."

Les says, "Clarence had a DeSoto car and he brought that thing up to the house in the back of his car. I think it cost less than fifty bucks."

Les's son Stuart, who also worked at Calef's as a young man, bought his Remington Model 700 there. That was back in the 1960s, Les says, before you had to have a federal firearms license. Guns had to be special ordered, but the ammunition was in stock. Les says, "There's a sign on the building that says, Get it at Calef's, and you could."

As Told by Les Waterhouse

Spunk

I was just a kid and was riding in to work with another guy. We were late. We didn't get here until five minutes past 8:00. Mr. Calef [Austin] was standing by the door. He said, to Gerry Newell, who I was riding with, he said, "Gerald, we begin at 8:00 here."

Gerry says, "Yuh, well we close at 6:00 and I was here 'til 6:30 last night."

Old Man Calef said, "We start at 8:00 and I expect you to be here." He disregarded the 6:30 part.

So later on that day, Gerry says to me, "If you want a ride be ready 'cause I'm leaving here at 6:00."

I said OK.

Came 6:00 I was ready and out the door we went.

Harlan got very upset. Not with me but with Gerry.

So the next day I overheard a conversation between Harlan and his father. He told his father that he should discipline Gerry because he left with the store full of customers.

The Old Man said, "I like that boy. He's got spunk."

End of subject.

Joelism —"Kick-em." As in: "The store's full of customers, it's ten minutes to closing time, everybody's tuckered out, but no letting down now. Time to buckle down, move fast, run the checkout like the wind, keep smiling, and, in general, kick-em."

At Calef's, like other country stores, you could not only buy what you needed, but sell what you had excess of—eggs, vegetables, bird houses, doughnuts. Here you met your neighbors, caught up on the goings-on, and even collected your mail —depending on whether the federal administration was Democrat or Republican. Calef's leaned Democrat.

"Mostly locals way back," Joel says. "I knew everybody's name came in here. Well, chalk it up now. I don't know mor'n half of'em. And some of 'em I don't want to. Used to be way back, sure, they came in on a regular basis. At the register, they had a container with a flip top and kept all the slips in there for what people owed. Quite a few had a running slip. I guess they'd come in every week or something and pay what they could."

On a Saturday night, you could put on your dancing shoes and boogie. "Upstairs," Joel says, "where Edward Jones is now, it was a dance hall. They had grange meetings and socials up there because that was the whole idea of it. Calef's would put on different things for the people in town to come to. They'd set up chairs around the edge and have a dance." The town gave Calef's their patronage and Calef's gave back to the town.

"Do you like to dance, Joel?" I asked.

"I didn't go to the dances, no. I do the barnyard shuffle and that's about it."

Joelism —"Chalk it up." As in: "I don't know a thing about dancing the jitterbug or the hully gully or the Watutsi. Can't do it. Won't do it. Chalk it up."

In many ways Calef's remains the center of town or at least one of the centers—Barrington's pretty sprawly and spread out. Locals stop in for coffee, sandwiches, a homemade salad from the deli, or the week's supply of Snappy Old Cheese. They stop in to catch up on the news or spread it. Gossip? Well, gossip is just news that hasn't yet been fully substantiated, and is all the more interesting for it. Folks stop in for a smile and a hello and to see what's new on the shelves or cooking in the pot.

They come from all over. It's both a local hang out and a tourist destination, or at least a stopover on the way to the ocean or the mountains or Grandma's house. Kids make a bee-line for the penny candy corner—Boston Baked Beans (remember those red-coated sweets?), nonpareils (chocolate with sprinkles), NECCO Wafers (the mints spark in the dark), Goo Goo Clusters. Most of the penny candies now cost five cents, but there's still one jar where each piece costs just a penny. It's tradition.

"We had candy, you know, the chocolates," Joel says. "We had to test it for the people to make sure it was good. I kinda liked those old fashioned chocolate drops. Ox hearts. Cream center. Oh my God, lickin' good you know. I have quite a few favorites. I like the Bit-O-Honey, but I love the Pepmint Patties."

"And yet," I say, "you maintain your youthful figure."

"I got to do that because I'm out in the public."

"What do you do to stay slim? What's your regimen, Joel?"

"I'm out back cuttin' cheese."

Soup and bread mixes are almost as popular as the candies. As are dried beans—a perennial favorite. Probably goes without saying that Joel is full of beans. He names them off like old friends:

- The California pea.
- The navy bean—a little bigger than the California pea, same family.
- Jacob's cattle—a best seller.
- The yellow eye.
- The pinto.
- The soldier bean—very popular.

19

- The cranberry bean—kinda tasty, reddish, a little spotty, looks like a cranberry.
- Red kidney—no matter what, left or right kidney, it's still good.
- And the sulphur bean (pronounced sulfa).

Pile 'em high, watch 'em fly: that's the motto of the country store. And always keep a good supply of dry beans on hand.

Joel says: "The sulfa beans have a taste all their own. I don't care for that one, but a lot of people like it. We sold a lot of beans. Customers come in and say, 'Hey, Saturday night. Bean night. We gotta have our beans.'"

Over time the configuration of the store has changed and changed again. Early days, according to Les Waterhouse, the counters stretched the length and breadth of the store in a U shape. "The customer didn't go around and pick out what they wanted. They told you what they wanted and you went and got it for them." That kind of service continued into Joel's day. Certain customers expected clerks to find and fetch what they required, just as they always had—even though the full counter had been replaced by a smaller checkout at the front. Even though the shelves and bins and barrels and candy jars were open for customers to select and collect for themselves.

Joelism —"Ain't that a pissa." As in: "Upon hearing the latest tidbit of scandalous local gossip, Uncle Pete said, 'Ain't that a pissa.'"

This saying comes from a longer one. "I hope your hat doesn't have any holes in it because it's a pissa." Meaning, "Nice hat."

As Told by Joel

What Bertha Wants Bertha Gets

Bertha Hayes, very prominent lady in town, way back, used to live where Helen Musler lives now, Sunnyside. Bill Hayes, one of her sons, lived in Barrington. They'd go to New York in the winter. Very wealthy family. Well off, yuh. He kinda put together the Barrington Orioles ball team.

About twice a year, they'd put on a big bash for all the kids in town, Mother told me this. They'd go, and there'd be a big table covered with toys and each kid could go up and pick a toy that he liked. And then they had candy and ice cream.

Mother told me they would come hoss and buggy from New York. I guess about eight or nine carriages. Servants. Oh yuh. Her husband was wealthy. Money was no object. Mother said she'd see 'em coming like a caravan. They had lamps all up the lane to get to the house, at night all lit up. They had I guess about twelve or thirteen servants. It was really something.

In her later years Mrs. Hayes, she came in here to shop. Sure. She said to 'em, "I want Joel and only Joel to wait on me." You know I'd have to walk around with her. She'd want something and I'd have to go with her and show it to her. She'd say to me, "Now, where's your flour" or something like that and I'd have to go with her. That's how she done her shopping. Not like today, they go round and pick up everything they want. Oh no.

She was a very nice lady, but firm, and she wanted what she wanted.

At one time Calef's offered home delivery to those who needed it. Mostly these were elderly folks, homebound. They couldn't get to the store, so the store came to them.

"We had about fifteen families that would call in and place their orders," Joel says. "Usually it was Thursday, the day we'd deliver with the big truck. Bertha Ross worked in the office. She was the one that took the orders. The clerks had to put them together. Either Harlan would deliver or sometimes Roger. Once or twice they were kinda shorthanded and I had to go on the route, too. It was kinda fun. Every week the same people would give their order and we would deliver it to their house. Some were elderly people—Mrs. Critchet or Edna Smith or like that. We did that for many years. The roads were not the greatest. Some were still dirt."

Les Waterhouse was among those who drove the truck, even before Joel's time. Les said, "We delivered in Barrington up by Durgin Farm and then almost up to the Ridge in Northwood—that was the last customer. Then we went the other way down Route 4 to Nottingham, 'bout the Nottingham line. It took five or six hours. We delivered grain too. We used an International truck."

Barbara Waterhouse says her husband, Les, had wanted to drive truck since he was five. "He told his mother when he was small he was going to grow up and drive a truck."

"Yes," Les says, "My goal in life was to drive a truck."

"And he did," Barbara says, "Drove them for many years." Driving truck for Calef's was a good starter job. Later he went to work for a bigger company, drove truck for them, then became a dispatcher and terminal manager. Les told other drivers where to go. Made a career of it.

On the Calef's route, Les brought news and collected it. His son Dan says, "That was their social for the day—that's why they wanted deliveries." For the homebound, the grocery delivery might be their only contact with the outside world that day or that week. Calef's home delivery was an early version of Meals on Wheels.

Les described one pair of customers who always gave him a run for his money. "There were two old maid sisters. One of them was deaf as a steak. And the other one didn't want anything to do with transaction at all. Ella was the deaf one and the other one would holler to her, ELLA. It would pierce your ears just about. ELLA, THE GROCERIES ARE HERE. ELLA ELLA. Finally Ella would hear. She had a cigar box with money in it. She'd put it on the table and say OK there's your money. We took out whatever it was for the groceries. Dig around until you got the exact change."

"Did anybody every give you a tip, Les, when you delivered their groceries?" I asked.

He said, "Oh, they'd give you a tip all right. 'Get back in the truck.'"

Barbara added, "And don't back over the lawn."

Lester Waterhouse remembers Calef's *before* Joel.

Spinach & Cheddar Squares

Ingredients

- 3 eggs
- 1 cup flour
- 1 cup milk
- 1 teaspoon salt
- 1 teaspoon baking powder
- 2 packages thawed spinach
- 1 Tablespoon chopped onion
- 4 Tablespoons margarine
- 1 pound shredded Calef's Aged Cheddar

Directions

Mix together eggs, flour, milk, salt, and baking powder.

Once well mixed, add Cheddar, spinach, and onion.

Use the margarine to grease well a 9x13 pan and then add the remaining margarine to the mixture.

Pour the mixture into pan and bake at 350°F for 35 minutes.

Cut the mixture into squares for warm canapés or larger pieces for a lunch. You may freeze the Spinach Squares for reheating later.

≋ Chapter 3 ≋

Calef's Owners
Then and Now

B y now, if you're still reading—
and apparently you are—
you're probably wondering, who's
who. Austin, Clarence, Alberta,
Roger? How are they related?
Which generation are we talking about? Here, for your edifica-
tion and delight, is the rundown of
Calef's owners from the beginning:

Mary Chesley Calef started Calef's
Country Store in 1869 in the front room
of her country home in Barrington.

- Mary Chesley Calef
  mortgaged her farm and
  opened the store in 1869.
  She stocked goods and
  sold them out of the front
  room of her house at what
  is now known as Calef's
  Corner. She was a widow,
  just twenty-four years old.
  Later she would become
  the first Calef to be named
  postmaster.

A page from Mary's 1872 Ledger read as follows:

2 doz eggs 36¢

2 qts molasses 30¢

1 broom 30¢

one half barrel of flour $3

16 lbs Beef $2.25

2 men's shirts $1.30

1 pair shoes, $1.25

From an article by Ada Hayes in the *Shoreliner*, October 1950.

RE-ELECT

CALEF
Senator

**40 YEARS IN BUSINESS
AND A TAX PAYER**

HE HAS SERVED YOU WELL

NEW HAMPSHIRE SENATE
1933—1936

SENATOR CALEF
Served on
All Major Committees of the Senate:

Committee for RECONSTRUCTION of STATE GOVERNMENT
FINANCE Committee—(Clerk)—4 years
PUBLIC IMPROVEMENT Committee—4 years
NEW HAMPSHIRE UNIVERSITY Committee—4 years
TRANSPORTATION Committee—4 years—(Chairman)—2 years
FORESTRY Committee—2 years
Final Committee for DRAFTING LIQUOR LEGISLATION
JUDICIARY Committee—2 years
STATE BUILDING Committee—2 years
INSURANCE Committee—(Chairman)—2 years
SENATE DELEGATE to AMERICAN LEGISLATIVE ASSOCIATION—2 yrs.

Was NEITHER ABSENT NOR LATE during last two sessions

Among Senator Austin Calef's claims to fame: "Was neither absent nor late during the last two sessions."

- Mary's son, Austin Calef, a barber who would become a state
  senator and big cheese in state politics, took over the management in 1895. Austin served two terms in the NH Senate. He
  was asked to run for governor in 1939, but turned down the
  offer. Who knows what would have happened had he accepted?
  Instead, he concentrated on building the business. He built a
  new store beside the house and later expanded even further,
  adding the front section. A Democrat in a Republican town
  in a Republican state, as state senator, he finagled to get a road
  built to his store on the bed of the old Nashua, Rochester,
  Worcester Railway. That road is now known as the Calef
  Highway, named for Austin. Good for business? You betcha.

Les Waterhouse says: "Mr. Calef wasn't stupid. He got a road built right
to his store. He was a senator and he got that built through the legis-
lature. A Democrat in a Republican town. Some people weren't happy
about that. But they still came to his store. What choice did they have?
It was the only game in town."

As Told by Alberta Calef St. Cyr

Politics Through the Generations

When I first dated Roger Calef, his grandparents lived in the house
next to the store. That would be Austin and Clellie. They had a lot of
political connections. Austin's the one that put the road through.

I can remember going to several functions there. The lawn behind
that house at that time was a beautiful garden area. Austin would have
other people from the state over and they would entertain them. The
family would all be there. They would serve punch and cookies and
things like that. That would be my first remembrance of the family.
That would be 1947.

Austin Calef during the war was on the draft board. Anybody
who was going to be drafted, they'd say Austin Calef would be getting
in touch with them.

I always tried to talk Joel into being a Democrat but I didn't have any luck. The Calefs at that time were very strong Democrats, which was unusual in this town.

My father-in-law [Clarence Calef] dated Mildred Locke, who became his wife. Her family were Republicans. Back then they took these things very seriously. He always felt the Calefs didn't approve of Mildred. And the Lockes didn't approve of Austin.

- Austin's sons, A. Harlan Calef and Clarence Calef, gradually took over store management in the 1920s and 30s. Ada Hayes wrote about the enterprising brothers for the *Shoreliner*: "Clarence, a lad with a flair for advertising, wrote copy and mailed advertising bulletins to a mailing list of between 1300 and 1400 families. Harlan, at twelve or thirteen years of age, was buyer for the ice cream; the proceeds from which became their pocket money. Both boys, even then, put their hard-earned money back into the

Harlan Calef (pictured) and his brother Clarence started working at the store young. Maybe not quite this young, but young.

business and purchased a refrigerator for the store. At present [1950], the store maintains eight employees. The fact that an employee has never been fired is a source of great pride."

- Harlan's son, George, and Clarence's son, Roger, worked alongside their fathers. When Joel started in 1957 at age seventeen, he was still in high school. High school was not his favorite activity. But work at Calef's suited him just fine. At that time George and Roger had some management duties, but Clarence and Harlan were still running the show. "I liked Clarence and Harlan," Joel says. "You had to pay attention and stay busy. If you didn't they'd speak to you. They'd say, 'Let's get on with it.' They didn't have to say it too many times."

Clarence retired in 1967. Roger died in 1984.

Alberta Calef, Roger's wife, then became manager. Her children and grandchildren (the 6th and 7th generations of Calef's involved with the store) helped out.

As Told by Alberta Calef St. Cyr

Romance Blooms in Barrington

Calef's had special meaning for me ever since I was a child. They sold ice cream just in the summer, not in the winter. You were very excited when you could get an ice cream cone at Calef's. I never thought I would be so involved.

It was after World War II. I never had known Roger. Although I probably had bumped into him at times because he delivered groceries back then. My grandparents lived at a farm at the corner of 9 and 202. My grandfather had cows—he had about nineteen, if I remember right. And my mother was divorced, which was almost unheard of back then. This was the thirties. She lived with her parents and that's where my childhood was.

I remember Leon Calef and his wife Arlene held a Halloween party in Leon's chicken barn. They'd cleaned it out. It was all decorated, live music. They invited the whole town. Anyone was to come to this party. Of course you realize the town probably wasn't more than three thousand people. Not everybody knew Leon Calef but most of them did.

You were supposed to wear a costume. I didn't wear a costume. I made my sister Gloria a costume out of the *Rochester Courier*. I sewed the paper together and made her dress. I didn't have time for me. I wasn't going to stay I didn't think.

So I went down to the party and Roger Calef had just come home from the war. His father had bought him a new car, brand new DeSoto. Course it was the highlight of the night. Everybody wanted to see it. We hadn't seen any new cars.

I remember that I met Roger that night. He was five years older. I was so impressed with him. But I don't think he hardly noticed me.

I used to wait at the store for my ride to the high school. We didn't have any transportation. You had to arrange your own. And I would walk from my house to the store. Roger would come out and talk to me while I was waiting for my ride. But he had a girlfriend down in West Newbury, Mass. I remember at Christmas he bought her skis and he wanted to try them up against me, because he thought we were about the same height. But anyway, I was—I'm sure—falling in love with this person.

That February we had a huge snowstorm. Calvin Swain called me and said he was going to have a sleigh ride with his horses. Course we didn't plow back then like we do now. He said he was going to take all the teenagers. So would I go to the store and buy hot dogs and rolls so that we'd have a cookout.

I said yes.

I went down to the store and Roger wanted to know what I wanted with all these hot dogs. So I told him all about the sleigh ride. He wanted to know if anybody could come. And I said yes. He showed up. That really began our attention to each other.

As Told by Alberta Calef St. Cyr

How Joel Happened to Start Working at the Store

We delivered groceries. Two routes. Clarence Calef, Roger's father, he used to take groceries up to Joel's mother, up to Flora. He knew that she was very concerned, afraid that Joel wouldn't finish high school. She told him, you know, that Joel was very shy. So Clarence said, "Well, he needs to work at the store."

My father-in-law gave the store a little talking to. They were to help this person out and there wasn't to be any wisecracking. They'd lose their job if they stepped out of line.

When Joel started, he just stocked shelves. He wouldn't speak to anybody and if anybody came to speak to him, he'd kinda turn the other way as if he was busy.

But he started listening to the young guys and all their talk. The first thing you knew he would sorta laugh at these things. And before you knew it he was joining in. He liked playing tricks with them!

- In 1996 Alberta, after much soul searching, sold the store to Cleve and Lindy Horton, entrepreneurs from California. The rumor around town was that they were millionaires. Lindy assures me they weren't. The store had been owned and run by the Calef family for five generations, seven if you count Alberta's children and grandchildren who helped out in the final months before the sale.

Alberta explains: "When you have three children, after a while there isn't enough money in the store for that many families. There's me. There was my daughter working there. She was a single mum. She had no support at all. She had to have a job. Bill, who had given up his job and came to help. And then there was my son Jere, who always loved the store. The store couldn't support us all. Couldn't do it."

31

(L to R) Andrea Calef, her mother Alberta, and Joel share a laugh. Alberta sold the store out of the Calef family with regret in 1996.

She adds this hard truth as further explanation for why the family had to let the store go: "I may as well say it—I think the generation before Roger's took too much money out of the business. Right after the war, the store was booming. But instead of leaving money at the end of a year, they took it out and divided it among themselves, the two brothers, Clarence and Harlan. At that time there wasn't much to do but go to Calef's. The air base was down there and, boy, we were booming. But once all these other things started opening up, there were a lot of places to go to and a lot of things to do. The supermarkets. Gas stations. And the economy went down. In my mind we just had to sell the store. Plus I had a heart attack. Heart surgery. The time had come."

The contract between Alberta and the Hortons specified that Joel was to be kept on. He was to retain his job no matter what. He was part of the deal because he had, for so long, been such an important part of Calef's.

Turns out the Hortons didn't mind at all. Happy to have him. Joel knew everything there was to know about running the store. He provided institutional memory—what and who had come before, and how that worked out. The word invaluable comes to mind. Joel's experience was and is priceless. He won't say so. But others will.

32

Joelism —"Set you back a week." As in: "When Billy Calef sat Joel down and told him the store was to be sold out of the family, well, that set him back a week."

Lindy Horton and her husband Cleve, both native to New England, left their jobs in California to come home and work for themselves. Calef's, which Lindy had visited often as a child, happened to be for sale—for the first time in a hundred seventeen years give or take. Right store, right time, and a loan from the Small Business Administration: the stars aligned and Lindy and Cleve were in business in Barrington. "We examined every different mom and pop operation," Cleve said in an article published in the *Dover Times*, August 28, 1997. "And running a country store was one we thought we could do." Calef's, he said, "is a place people view as a destination. People walk in here and there's a step back in time." He hoped that he and Lindy could help bring Calef's back to "pre-eminence," back to a time when "cheese-buying customers were lined up out the door on a Sunday afternoon and visiting the store was an event." On the other hand, "We don't want to run a museum. We want a successful retail operation, with charm and atmosphere."

In a 1997 article in the *Boston Globe* by Rachel Collins, Cleve said, "Collectors want to know if the antiques and old artifacts are up for sale. I say, No. That would be like eating our seed corn."

Cleve Horton (front center) poses with Joel and the gang for the Fourth of July.

Calef's has had financial ups and downs in its 150 years. The store, like our state and our country, went through busts and booms. But Calef's never lost track of its mission: Small store, small town, provide what's needed, attend to detail, remember and appreciate your place in the community, give gracious service always.

For the last sixty years, Joel has been the constant. He says, "My mother asked Clarence if he'd take me on. He said, 'Yuh, we'll give him a try.' I'd come in after school and stock shelves. I've been here ever since."

Alberta says: "I was very sad that we had to part with the store. I wanted to make sure that Joel…." She trails off, then picks up again. "Anybody we ever talked to about buying the store we said they had to keep Joel." She adds, "Way back there is a little connection to the Calefs with the Sherburnes, family wise."

By way back, she means way back. Both families count many generations in New Hampshire, deep old gnarly roots. So it's no surprise that, at some point, the family trees cross-pollinated. The Sherburne House, the oldest house at Portsmouth's historic Strawbery Banke Museum, belonged to a branch of Joel's family. It was built somewhere around the turn of the century, the 18th century that is.

In 2012, Greg Bolton and Len Angelo bought the store from the Hortons. Greg manages the store today. Len acts as silent partner. Alberta is a big fan of Greg's management and how the store is updated but still faithful to what it used to be. "Greg has a happy store," she says. "And that's one of the things that pleases me."

Destination Calef's

Margie Shepard Walker, when she found out this book was in the making, wrote: "When I was a kid it was a big treat to take the long drive up 125 from South Lawrence, MA, to Calef's. We always would get cheddar cheese with a box of crackers and donut holes. We would make the trip usually in the fall to see the leaves (going way up North) and then again in the spring."

≋ Chapter 4 ≋

A True Country Store

What makes a true country store?

It's a combination of a lot of elements. A true country store carries a variety of goods, including some things that might not at first seem to fit together—like penny candy and hot sauce, or books by local authors (like me) and three sizes of firkins, AKA cheese boxes, all marked with the Calef's logo. Like homemade doughnuts and 1000-piece jigsaw puzzles.

The true country store is locally owned, staffed, patronized, and appreciated. A lot of kids from town get their first work experience there, so they develop an early and life-long loyalty. Joel says, "We've had about every kid in town work here at one time or another. The family would come in and say, 'Can't you give him a job?'"

Some of the young kids work just a few summers while they're in school. But Joel says, "Some stayed right heah. You're lookin' at it!"

When you walk into a true country store, the setting feels familiar, even if you've never set foot in it before. The true country store feels welcoming, homey, old-timey, and, yes, a little kitschy. Who can resist a can of cocoa mix with a label featuring Lucille Ball in a chef's hat? Not me. Or a plastic moose that poops jelly beans? Gotta have it.

The true country store smells good too—fresh baked bread, cinnamon, hot apple cider, molasses, and coffee. Maybe there's a hint of age in the air—the dust of a century and a half settled into the cracks.

If the front door creaks a bit and looks like it's been used and abused for decades, that's because it has. The glass in the windows is thin and a little filmy, the window frames and cross pieces thick with layers of paint. Billy McGowan painted Calef's sprawling store some years ago. He remembers that it took "ninety-two gallons for the outside. Cream colored. I had a couple helpers." While he was at it, he painted the inside, too.

Joel says, "You done the store, the house, the whole thing. Yuh, you brushed up on your work."

In the true country store, some of the shelves sag in the middle, as though the heavy loads of the past were almost—not quite—too much for them. The floorboards, dark with the patina of age, dip and rise from the uneven wear of foot traffic.

Change, when it comes, comes slowly. If your favorite brand of oyster cracker is on a certain shelf in a certain spot one day, it'll be there the next day and the next. You can depend on it. Your favorite clerk will be on hand to wait on you today, tomorrow, and, in a lot of cases, ten years from now. The employees are as loyal as the patrons.

Today's true country store is, fundamentally, the same as the country store fondly recalled from childhood. I remember Hod Hastings Store in Danbury, New Hampshire, and my grandfather, Robert Stewart, sitting on an upended apple box, shooting the breeze with his buddies including my great-uncle L. E. Ford. (We called him L. E., though his name was Lawrence Eliot.)

My grandparents had no car, Hastings was within walking distance—down street, which meant down a hill, past the church, and across Route 4. All the food they didn't grow or produce at home (vegetables, apples, milk and butter from the two cows, pork from the two annual pigs), they bought at Hastings Store. Walking into Calef's brings those memories back to me.

"It's the atmosphere," Joel says. "I don't know how many people will come in this store and they will open the door and they just can't believe it. They will say, 'Oh my gosh, this takes me back so many years.' We try to keep it the same as it's always been. They hear about it and they want to look at it. The new owners, they haven't changed it hardly any, only what they had to do. I don't know how many have said to me, 'Why, Joel, we just can't believe it.' And they'll smile all over their face."

Many true country stores in New England still have a wood stove, centrally located, and put to good use come cold weather. Practicality rules. The stove gets stoked and its warmth draws chilled customers with outstretched hands. Next to the stove at Calef's, the wooden table where Joel and I enjoyed for our weekly chats, provides a cozy place to sit and drink a hot beverage or a tonic (known in other parts of the country as soda or pop) or eat a sandwich. Cleve Horton,

CANDIDATE STASSEN, working hot-stove circuit, tries his hand at the folksy approach.

Calef's hosted many political figures over the years. Harold Stassen ran for president ten times between 1948 and 1992. We're guessing this is an early run. Stassen adds fuel to the fire, flanked by Harlan Calef and Al Wood.

when he and Lindy owned the store, used to keep a price tag on the table, though it wasn't really for sale. The store isn't licensed as a sit-down eatery, but people will sit down and eat—on an overturned apple box if necessary. At some point the price tag disappeared. The table remains, a place to take a load off and visit or just sit quietly contemplating your place in the universe. In warm weather, there's seating on the porch—or on the steps for that matter. Nobody stands on ceremony at Calef's.

As Told by Alberta Calef St. Cyr

Jack Bodge and the Wood Stove

Roger was fifty-nine when he died. I had him in and out of Mass General. It was a terrible time. My son Bill was working for Sprague Electric when he got through college. But when his father got sick he came back and helped with the store.

The town, they were awfully good. They brought food.

There was a man in town called Jack Bodge. He was a character. He tipped the bottle quite badly. Roger always told Jack that if he had too much to drink, he was to call Roger and Roger would go get him and take him home.

Roger died in July. The first of it getting cold in the fall, the only heat we had in the store was the stove out front and a coal stove in the back. The meat crew would stock up the coal stove. Here I am trying to run that wood stove.

So the first really cold morning, Jack Bodge showed up probably about 7:15. I usually went up about that time because the store opened at 8:00. I had a lot to do. Jack showed up and he started the stove for me. He said he was doing it for Roger. Jack showed up every morning and started that stove until Jack Bodge himself passed on. I couldn't believe it. That was the stove out front.

That's an example of the town helping out.

I loved Jack Bodge and I know Roger did.

Dr. Jo Laird stops by most every morning for coffee and a muffin. This has been her habit for years. She's as much fixture as the Coca Cola cooler on the porch or the red phone in the corner. She lives in Strafford and teaches geology at UNH. "She's between a rock and a hard place," Joel says.

One of the characteristics of Yankee humor—I know this because I'm a licensed Yankee humorist—is that you don't know if the Yankee means a comment to be funny or serious. You certainly can't tell from his face or from his even tone. Deadpan. Pokerfaced. Cards close to the chest, perhaps tucked in the pocket of a buttoned to the neck flannel shirt. Or in Joel's case, tucked in the pocket of his white butcher's apron.

Joel typically greets Dr. Jo with this question, "How's your day going to be?"

She answers, "Not too bad, but don't ask about tomorrow." She likes teaching, but she doesn't enjoy meetings. Maybe "tomorrow" is a day for meetings. For years she's been threatening to retire. "But she goes right back," Joel says.

"What brings you into Calef's so often?" I asked Dr. Jo, thinking the draw might be quality of the coffee or muffins, the friendly atmosphere, fresh news, or all of the above. I should have anticipated her dry-as-bone reply. She spoke, as she always speaks, low, slow and with precision. She stops at Calef's each morning, she says, because "it's halfway between home and work."

"Dr. Jo, you and Joel have a lot in common," I say.

"Yes," she says, low, slow and with precision. "We do."

A true country store not only has character, but its fair share of characters. Joel's wicked sense of humor continues the tradition of a long line of jokesters, Harlan Calef among them. Harlan was infamous for the tricks he liked to play on new employees. Rites of passage, you might say, like this one:

"I got something I want you to do today and see how well you are at doing it," Harlan would tell the newbie.

He had a funnel, Joel says, a little pitcher of water that he set on the counter, and a quarter. He'd say to the fella, "I want you to take this funnel and tuck it right down where your buckle is on your pants. Just slide it right down in. And I want you to lean your head back and put this quahtah on your nose. I want you to bend your head forward and have it drop in the funnel. Do you think you can do that?"

And the fella would say, "Yuh, I think so."

"Course they couldn't do it," Joel says. It was just about impossible. After a few tries Harlan would offer a little advice. "Well," he'd say, "all right. I'm gonna ask you to do it another time. But this time kinda shut your eyes and imagine you're at Niagara Falls. You've really gotta concentrate and picture yourself at Niagara Falls."

He'd take the pitcher of water, Joel says, "and turn some right down in the funnel. And oh my God. Course when that water hit, they come around, and the quahtah went right on the flo-ah."

Harlan was full of it, Joel says. "Oh God. He come out with some good ones."

Main Street, complete with street sign, is a passageway between the buildings. "A little alley," Joel says, "from the main store to the gift shop. Before it was a gift shop, they sold grain, duck food, all kinds of stuff."

For a while, way back, a string hung by the door, Joel said, "It just hung there and a lot of them would go out through and after a while it got to them. They had to pull it. And when they did they got a bucket of water on them." Courtesy of Harlan. Harlan enjoyed a good water prank.

As Told by Joel

The Infamous Bag Stretcher

We had different sized poly bags. When we had new clerks come in, we'd say, "Go out back and get a 4" by 2" by 12" bag and get the bag stretcher, cause you've got to stretch that out to a 6" by 3" by 15"."

We had a big shed out back with stock in it. They'd go out. And look. And they'd come back in and say, "We can't find any bag stretcher."

I'd say to them, "You've got to go out and find it. It's right out there and it says right on it what it is."

Well, they'd go out and look and they'd come back again.

Finally either Harlan or myself we'd kinda get irritated. We'd get ugly with them. Well, they'd go out and they'd come back with something, but it wasn't anything to do with a bag stretcher.

And then we'd tell them it was a joke. The was no such thing as a bag stretcher.

It worked good. It worked every time.

Joelism —"Don't that churn your buttah?" As in: "Winning $40 in the lottery. Don't that churn your buttah?" Good news churns a person's buttah. So does bad news, come to think of it. It something gets your attention and makes you feel good or bad, it churns your buttah.

One of the clerks asked Harlan for a special kind of candy. Chocolate. He didn't know the name of it, but it came in little squares wrapped in foil. So Harlan provided several squares wrapped in foil.

"The kid dove right into it." Joel says, "Oh lawdy."

After lunch the clerk had to make a run to the barn—the outhouse.

"How you doing?" Harlan asked after the clerk returned.

The clerk said, "I almost didn't make it. That come on me terrible."

"Terrible!" Joel says. "That clerk almost had to bank the curves."

The foil-wrapped squares weren't candy atall as it turns out, but ex-lax.

Joelism —"Bank the curves." When you have to get somewhere in a hurry, you might go so fast around the corner your wheels touch the bankings or even ride right along them. If you have to bank the curves, and you're not in a car race, you're in a rush to get somewhere for some particular pressing reason.

Of course, those who make jokes ought to be prepared to take them, and not get overly upset when the joke's on them. Harlan could take a joke. And so could his brother, Clarence.

Times gone by, Joel recalls, at the checkout counter they didn't have scotch tape or masking tape to seal a package. They tied the packages with string from a big wheel of twine cut to length as needed.

Clarence lived just down the road, within sight of the store. Each day he'd walk home for lunch.

One day, Joel says, "Somehow some of that twine got caught in his belt or pants or something and he didn't realize it. He said he was going home and would be back later on. There he goes out the store, and there's this string follering him down the road. Course at that time there was no lights here, just stop signs. Kept right on going, got right in the house. Finally, he gets home, he says, 'Oh my God, I left a trail.'"

Joel imagines that Mildred, Clarence's wife, probably said, "Well, you gotta know your way back so that's good. Cause you gotta go back

The wise customer Reverend Marshall Stevenson tastes the cheese before he buys it from Rudd Stevens.

after lunch to work some more." Instead of breadcrumbs like Hansel and Gretel, Clarence left a trail of twine.

"They kidded him good about that," Joel recalls. "That's for sure. I guess a few of the customers said, 'Why has Clarence got that string on to him?' That was quite a maneuver."

A true country store lives in stories that recall and bring to life the days when packages were tied with string, and when getting a bucket of water on the head, substituting ex-lax for chocolate, or persuading a young man to put a funnel down his pants was all in good fun. A country store lives in its people with their tricks and quirks and foibles. People fondly remembered. People still on the job. The true country store is an oasis of living history on the busy corner of routes 9 and 125 in a small New England town.

"The store was kind of a central point in town," Joel says. "If they wanted the news, what was going on, or if somebody had died or something, they could get the information here. Course way back they even had the post office here at the store. They even had the post boxes."

As Told by Joel

Where's Roger?

Years ago when Roger was here, he was kinda my boss at the time. Before the addition there was a back door. There was little shed out there. We kept the wheels of Rat Trap Cheddar, hundred-pound bags of dry beans, and also the paper bags.

We had an employee who had an MG. One of those little cars. He'd go out just before he was ready to go home and start that suckah to warm it up. Well, it made the worst noise you ever heard.

My job was to go out and lock the sheds before six o'clock. So about quarter of I'd go out and lock 'em.

I come back in and, my gosh, it got about quarter past six and somebody says, "Where's Roger?"

I said, "I don't know. I haven't see him atall."

Time passed and still no Roger. "Where's Roger?" they said. Somebody said, "He went out in the shed to count cheese." I said, "What time was this?"

They told me. I said, "Oh my God, I gotta go out. I think I've locked him in the shed."

Oh yes. It was dark. And I guess he knocked stuff over. And I went out and he's hollering, "Hey, can anybody hear me?"

And I said, "Roger, are you in there?"

"Yes," he says, "get me outta here."

You know, he thought I done it on purpose. Well, I didn't. I just didn't hear him holler with that stupid car going.

He didn't understand that at first. Not very well.

It took me quite a while to convince him that I didn't do it on purpose. He was out there quite a while. Thank God somebody in here says, "Where's Roger?" And I said, "Holy mackerel."

That darned car made such a racket. I never forgot it and he didn't either. I wouldn't have dreamed of locking him in the shed. It was an accident. Finally, he realized I didn't do it on purpose. But for awhile it was touch and go.

A true country store is not what's stocked on the shelves—that changes over time. Has to. When Lindy and Cleve Horton took over, they didn't want to sell meat, except deli meat for the sandwiches. George Calef Fine Foods, just down the road, has cornered the Barrington meat market in recent years. Yup, the same George Calef who worked with his cousin Roger at the big store set up a competing business in 1978. Alberta Calef says Roger "was very stressed when George decided to build the market." She says, "I think it was a competition that came down through the family. Clarence and Harlan were brothers, but they didn't always agree. Harlan was a very vocal person. Clarence was a very quiet person. Roger came on and George in the next generation, so it just seemed to carry on. They worked at getting along. That was about it."

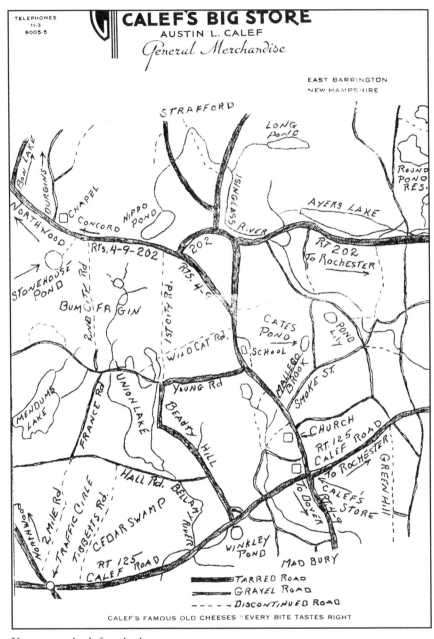

You can get theah from heah.

She adds, philosophically: "I'm friendly with George and I try to understand. I figure that was life. I wish though that my husband didn't spend the time he did worrying about it. But that's life."

And life goes on, day after day, customer after customer. When change rolls in—big or small—the wise store owner or employee rolls with it. Change may be excitin' as Joel says, but more often than not it's also bittersweet—something lost, something gained. "When Lindy and Cleve took over," Joel says, "we didn't even do the corned beef any more. George does it over next door. At one time, I cut all kinds of meat here. We'd hang the round up on the hook and break it down. If you do it that way, with the hook, it just kind of falls down. Gravity."

Behind the deli counter, the old meat hook still hangs from the ceiling. Calef's sold a lot of meat in its day. Joel says, "We had porter house, T-bone, top round, bottom round. We had a cube steak machine. You'd take the meat and run it through and tenderize it. Break down the fibers."

And in the small world department, he says, "Believe it or not, Lindy's father would come in here and buy cube steaks even before Lindy and Cleve bought the store. Years before. They didn't know it atall. Our cube steaks were wonderful. He'd come like every other week and get two or three pounds. He lived in Massachusetts."

The cube steak connection came to light sometime after Cleve and Lindy bought the store. Maybe at a family gathering. Something like, "You know that store you bought, Lindy, I used to go there all the time for cube steak."

"Really, Dad? All the way to Barrington, New Hampshire?"

"Really. They had the best cube steak around."

Eventually they sprung the coincidence on Joel. Lindy took him aside and said, kinda serious, "I gotta tell you something."

Joel said, "What have you gotta tell me?"

Lindy said, "For quite a while you waited on my dad."

Joel said, "I did?"

"Yes, do you remember the person that used to come in for the cube steaks?"

Joel said, "Yes, course I do."

She said, "That's my father."

Joel said, "My God."

Just then Lindy's father walked through front door. Surprise! A face from the past—cube steak man. Joel says: "He laughed, you know. And I said, For heavens sakes." What goes around comes around. And around. And around.

Joel says, "The one that really started it was Mary Chesley Calef, Austin's mother. Austin Calef, the barber, he was Clarence and Harlan's father. He lived in the big house over here with his wife Clellie. He had his office in a little cubby hole here at the store. Al Wood, he waited on the customers. He took care of the tonic. Al always had a pipe. He was very pleasant. Very nice to the customers. Friendly. 'Good morning, good afternoon, are you looking for something special?'"

Right now, Joel says, "I just love to come here and work—the atmosphere and the team that we have. And even back then, they worked with me and helped me to kind of blend in. The Calefs were really great to work for. And it's just like this today. We work together and do our thing and it all works out beautiful."

Joelism —"Run hard and put away wet." As in: "Twelve hours on the job makes a fella feel like he's been run hard and put away wet."

≡

Pure New Hampshire maple syrup is always a good seller.

Mary Calef Cheese Soup

Ingredients

- 6 ounces Calef's Aged Cheddar grated
- 6 ounces Rat Trap Cheddar grated
- 4 Tablespoons butter
- ½ cup diced carrot
- ½ cup diced green pepper
- ½ cup minced onion
- ½ cup minced celery
- ½ cup flour
- 1 quart well-seasoned chicken stock
- 3–4 cups fresh milk
- salt and white pepper

Directions

1. Melt butter in double boiler, add vegetables.
2. Braise vegetables until tender, not brown.
3. Blend in flour. Cook one minute, stirring constantly.
4. Add stock and cook; stir until thick.
5. Add Cheddars; stir until they melt.
6. Thin with milk to creamy consistency.
7. Season with salt & pepper.
8. Strain, Reheat in double boiler.
9. Serve hot—or in warm weather, serve very cold.

≋ Chapter 5 ≋

Run Hard
and Put Away Wet

Running a country store is hard work. Constant. Unrelenting. All consuming. You name it. So much hard work done for so long accounts in part for why the store was sold out of the Calef family. The work itself, over the generations, took its toll. Alberta Calef St. Cyr says, "My family would hate for me to say this, but that next generation didn't want to work as hard as the generations before. Seven days a week. Roger couldn't go to anything when my kids were in school. He was working all the time. My kids [after they grew up] wanted to spend time with their families." And who can blame them?

Real Joel checks out a banner with a photo of bigger-than-life Joel on the occasion of his fiftieth anniversary of working at the store. Calef's rarely misses an opportunity to celebrate.

Joel thrived on the work and the routine. He worked all kinds of hours. Still does. Still comes in at five every morning, bright eyed, bushy tailed, and ready to cut the cheese. He puts the coffee on. Gets the store set up to open its doors at 8:00 a.m. He stays, usually, until 11:00 a.m. It's a routine, but never boring, he says: "Every day I learn something different, and it's a challenge and I like it."

Used to be the store was open until nine in the evening on Fridays and Saturdays. Joel would be on hand to close up shop. Even if he'd started at dawn. Sometimes he went home for a rest in the middle of the day, but those were long days that led to the nights he felt as though he'd been "run hard and put away wet."

Whatever he was asked to do, he did. Without complaint. Day after day. Week after week. Year after year. "Some jobs," he admits, "were more excitin' than others. But we done it. Had to do it."

He started out stocking shelves, but before long was promoted to bagging. "Harlan kind of took me aside and said: 'I want you to start bagging stuff. You're good. You're fast. And I like it.' So I said all right."

In those days, most products came in bulk. The bulk had to be broken down, counted out by hand, packaged, and shelved for sale. "We used to package a lot of items," Joel says. "Cookies, crackers, chocolates. Old-fashioned chocolate drops. Oh my gosh, molasses cookies, Mary-Ann cookies. Nabisco. We sold a mess of them. They don't even make 'em today. They had the big cookies. Cartwheels they called them. No more of those. They had these coconut bar cookies with the creases on the top. Those were a big seller. Oh my God, dry beans. I bagged everything. And I done that for quite a while."

Later he received another promotion to the meat department, where he was known as "quite a cut-up."

Ed Douglas taught him the way around a slab of beef. "He had Douglas Market on Washington Street in Dover years ago. Well, he sold that and he come out here part-time. He showed me a lot of different cuts and everything." It was from Rudd Stevens that Joel learned never to use a dull knife—an important lesson. "Dangerous," Joel says. "With a dull knife, you're forcin' it." More likely to slice off a finger with a dull knife than a sharp one. Joel kept his knives well-honed and steeled. And his fingers intact.

The younger ones loved to watch him sharpen his knives, he says. "Like a lot of things, it excites 'em."

Occasionally, some of the young ones got a little too excited. Out back, on Main Street, a couple of them got to fooling around with those razor sharp knives. They practiced their knife throwing skills on the door. "Oh, they done that for quite a while," Joel says. "They'd have a little contest to see who could hit the door."

This kept them entertained until the day Harlan opened the door unexpectedly, just about a second after the knife penetrated the wood. "That ended the knife throwing," Joel says. Harlan told the boys, "My God, man. I don't ever want to see that happen again." The knife just missed him. "Would have gone right into him," Joel says. "They used to get fooling around. Some of the younger ones in the meat counter, yes."

As Told by Joel

Molasses

We used to pump our own molasses from a drum. Hand pump went down into the drum and you'd crank it. Oh, big suckah.

The drums would come in by tractor trailer. Fancy Barbados Molasses. They hauled it in on the back of the pickup and, one day, they didn't put the tailgate up. They got out here on Route 9 and that suckah slid right off that truck. Wonder it didn't hit somebody coming up through in a car.

Thank God it didn't break.

We had a clerk in here and he was pumping a gallon of molasses for somebody. You know in the summertime we see quite a few sights. Some we don't forget, cause they're kinda overwhelming.

Like an outfit from the Bill Blass collection, a famous designer, Bill Blass. Oh yes. He come out with something that was like wearing nothing atall. And some come in wearing that and you didn't really have to guess.

This clerk was pumping molasses, not paying attention, and this girl come in in a bikini and that's all it took. He kept his eyes right on her. Finally somebody says, "Hey, you better check your molasses." My God, he had it all over the top of the barrel, all over the floor. What a mess. Cause that girl distracted him. Course.

She looked just as good going as she did coming.

Joelism —"Don't that flush your toilet?" A pleasant surprise like a pretty girl in a bikini might flush your toilet. An unpleasant surprise like gallons of molasses spreading across the floor might also be said to flush your toilet. It's a versatile expression.

On a Saturday or a Sunday when the store was packed and Joel had to make his way through the hubbub, he'd call out, "Room for the feet! Room for the feet!" That seemed to do the trick. Sometimes he'd entertain colleagues by playing the Hawaiian air guitar. "Yuh," Joel says, "once in a while I think I'm on the island."

I asked if he would demonstrate. "No," he said, "I don't think so."

"I heard you used to bong like Big Ben at closing time. Would you do a few bongs for old times' sake?"

"That bong has long gone."

But he adds, "I also did bird calls. I was very good with my ruby red-breasted flow suckah. Have you ever heard of that, Becky? They're very rare."

Joel's colleagues will tell you he kept them entertained. Still does. He has a lot of fun kidding around with customers, too. "Some take it pretty good," he says. "Some don't."

The way people keep coming back, it seems most take it pretty good. One school teacher in particular enjoyed the homemade sausage,

Working hard at the counter. Some days the store was so crowded there was hardly enough space to "make room for the feet."

ground and spiced on site. "Boy, we sold a lot of it," Joel says. "We'd dish it out. They'd take a pound, two pounds. They'd go home and make patties."

Alberta Calef St. Cyr remembered that school teacher well: "She liked to put on a show and she loved Joel! When she came into the store and asked for sausage, she had a certain way of doing it. 'Joel,' she'd announce, 'I need some sausage.' It was quite a production."

On one occasion she made a particularly flamboyant production of her request. She danced in and waved her arms. "Joel," she sang out across the store, "I need some sausage."

Joel said, "Would you go outside and make that entrance one more time? It was so good."

So she did. The store was busy, but in she danced for a second time, even more flamboyant than before. Now she had everyone's attention. "Joel," she sang out, "I need some sausage."

There was a dramatic pause. Then Joel said, "Sorry, ma'am. We don't have any sausage today. I just sold the last of it."

Joelism —"Room for the feet." Instead of, "I'm coming through with cheese that somebody out front needs right now. Get out of the way," you say, "Room for the feet!" and the waters part.

As Told by Joel

The Lady and the Cabbage

Way back, when you came through the doah, we had a vegetable counter. We had produce. All kinds of produce. Customers would grab a turnip or a bag of apples and bring it out back to the counter for me to weigh.

This lady come in one day and she had a big rimmed hat on. It was starting in on summer. Well, she picked out a big head of cabbage. And she gave it to the clerk out front. He tried to bring it back out to me to get me to weigh it on the scale. But the stoah was so crowded he couldn't get through. So he said to me "Would you weigh this cabbage?"

I said I would.

He threw that cabbage across the stoah. He thought he'd done it high enough to miss her. But no, she had her head down lookin' at something, and it hit the rim of her hat, turned that suckuh right around. Spun it right around.

She never knew it atall. No.

I caught the cabbage. Weighed it and threw it back to him.

Yuh. She never knew what hit her. He says to me after, "That was a close one wa'n't it?"

Not all country stores have a big porch for sitting and chatting and displaying outdoorsy goods, but Calef's does. "We used to put everything on the porch," Joel says. "Way back when Harlan and Clarence and Roger were here, they had the box truck that they used to deliver with. They would go every two weeks to Boston to get a load of groceries. We'd have to take 'em off the truck and put 'em on the shelf. In the morning that truck was full of other stuff that we put on the porch. Anything from tires to fishing gear. It took us about a half an hour to take the stuff off the truck and put it on the porch. The whole front of the porch was covered. Yes."

At night, they repeated the onerous procedure in reverse. Pack it all back into the truck. They didn't keep anything out on the porch overnight, Joel says, except "the railway express wagon, which is still right out here at the end of the store."

Some seasonal merchandise, flowers and bird feeders and so forth, stayed out overnight covered with a tarp. "I remember some nice baskets they used to sell for pies," Joel says. "Wooden baskets. You could put two pies in 'em. A little shelf in it and a cover. We'd lug the stuff out and put it out there and bring it in at night. They done that for many years. Then they decided not to put so much on the porch. It got to be too much. Why they had cemetery urns and all kinds of stuff. You name it. They had it."

When Cleve and Lindy Horton bought the store, "They backed off putting so much stuff on the porch. A little bit but not like they used to."

In the spring, Calef's did and does sell plants from local growers like Larry Robie of Robie's Greenhouse. Sometimes the plants even made their way inside. One time two or three ivy plants ended up on the meat counter. A customer expressed interest.

Another celebration. This time it's the 125th anniversary of the founding of the store.

"She's lookin' 'em all over," Joel says, "and feeling 'em all over." She asked Joel if he knew about plants.

He said he did, sort of. "I don't overdo it."

She says, "What kind of an ivy is this anyway?"

"Gee," he said, "I think they told me it was poison."

Joel says, "She changed color quick. She was kinda rosy cheeked when she come in. When I told her about the ivy, set her back a week. I had some fun with it."

Yup, as Arlo Gurthrie said of Alice's Restaurant, used to be you could get anything you wanted at Calef's Country Store—and maybe even some things you don't want, like ivy of the pretend poison variety.

Roberta Robie, Larry's wife, made fresh doughnuts for the store. She also, on one occasion, helped Joel out with a very special request as follows.

As Told by Joel

Roberta's Television Cake

I met Milton Berle up at the Gilford Playhouse. I took Mother, cause she liked him, too. I bet I was back stage a half hour talking with him. He knew about Calef's because people had sent him cheese from here and he thought it was terrific!

Roberta Robie, who used to make the doughnuts here, well she also made cakes. I asked her would she make a cake that looked like a television, because, you know, he went by Mr. Television. She made me the most beautiful sheet cake and it looked just like a television. She got big round candy which looked like knobs on the television. And she wrote right on the screen, Mr. Television.

Well, I had it in the trunk. And his manager come out and I said, "I got a cake here, too." And I took it out and he said, "Oh my God." They took pictures of it. He said, "Oh, Milton is gonna love that!"

I went back stage, and they said to him, "Milton, look at this."

He thought it was awesome.

56

It was half white and half chocolate. She done a good job with that cake. That was probably twenty or twenty-five years ago. I'll never forget it. He was so nice to talk to. Back stage he was altogether different than on stage. I told him about Mother and where we were sitting.

The show was about ready to start cause it was Intermission, and, of course Mother had to go to the restroom. That's normal. So when he comes out he says, "I can't start until this lady comes back and gets in her seat."

When she comes down the aisle, he says, "Here she is now. Now when she gets in her seat, by God, we're gonna start the show."

And she coulda killed him. Everybody was lookin' and everything. He was awesome. Never forget it. Milton Berle.

It wasn't just his work at the store that made Joel feel sometimes as though he'd been run hard and put away wet. Despite working full time and, for many years, taking care of his mother—who lived to be 99 and a half—he took on many civic projects. Many.

When he noticed that Barrington didn't have a town seal, he designed one, went to the selectmen with his idea, got hold of an artist to put his design into shape. And before you knew it, Barrington had a town seal.

He founded the Barrington Ambulance Service. "The first ambulance," Joel says, "we done fundraising and got help from the town. We did shows and raffles and everything. It was a small ambulance but brand new. I still have that plaque that George give me—SHERBIE. On the front of the ambulance. Those were the days."

Yup, the first ambulance in Barrington was named SHERBIE, after Joel."

Luckily, Joel's work with the emergency services and his work at the store were a natural fit. Calef's was one of the first places in town to have a telephone. The red phone, still in place though no longer in use, rang for emergencies—a fire, an accident, or somebody needed help. From that red phone, volunteers—usually women who worked at home and could be depended on to answer—would be alerted and they, in turn, called firefighters and directed them to the scene. Calef's was emergency-call-central, and these stay-at-home women were the original volunteer dispatchers.

As Told by Joel

Filling a Need

I was a founder of the Barrington Emergency Medical Service. I will tell you how that happened. As far as medical calls, they were handled by the fire department, resuscitator calls. Course the training was very limited those days. I took a first aid course in Rochester with Bob Wallingford, one of the firemen there. And then I took the advanced first aid course. He said to me one day, he said, "Joel, your ability and how you put things across, you would make an excellent instructor." He said, "I'm going to put your name in."

I said, "Oh, you think I can do that?"

He said, "I know you kin. You can ad lib and it's wonderful."

He sent my name in and I took the instructor's course. I taught first aid and CPR with the American Red Cross.

Also, I was looking into EMT, emergency medical technician. I took the second course offered in the state of NH and passed it.

One day they had a medical call here in Barrington. The family discovered the woman two days after she'd fallen down in the cellar. The family, they were very irate. They called the fire department (after the family found her) and they helped her.

The selectmen called me to a meeting. Things had to change. They said, "Where we're very limited with medical services and where you've just had this EMT course, we'd like to have you go on calls and see if we can get an ambulance service in the town here." They said, "We are going to give you a title, Coordinator of Emergency Medical Services. Would you do that for us?"

I said, "Yes. I'll try and do it."

So they give me the title and I went to Benoit Medical Service which was Irving Benoit at the time. I talked with him because he had an ambulance service. At that time we had the Rochester Fire Department or we had the funeral home come out. They put a red light on the top of the hearse and it was an ambulance. Take the red light off and it was a hearse again. They'd just put 'em in the hearse, put the red light on, and go as fast as they could to the hospital.

I set up a first aid course in town here and got quite a few to do it. And then I said I'd like to set up a group and we'll have a first responder unit. For about three years I would go on a call and answer it myself. People would call me at home and whatever. I had my car and that was it. The ladies up here at the Mobile Home Estates put on a bake sale and got me a kit to carry in the car. Also Irving Benoit put a kit together for me.

Joel presents 2006 EMT of the year award to Nick Roun as Tony Maggio looks on. The first ambulance in the town of Barrington was nicknamed "Sherbie," after Joel Sherburne.

I'd get calls at night or in the morning early and I'd have to go and stabilize the patient or whatever. Then I formed the Emergency Medical Service Association. That was 1978.

One thing led to another. They promoted me. I was district chairman. With the American Red Cross, I was chapter chairman and first aid coordinator for many years.

They were very good here at the store. If we had a medical call or an ambulance call I could go and leave. No questions asked.

Joel taught and mentored many of the EMTs who served Barrington and beyond. Craig Deady, who currently serves as a member of the Barrington Emergency Services had this to say about his first meeting with Joel and life in a small town:

"The first time I met Joel was May of 2011. He was presenting me with my first EMT of the year award. I was humbled by his knowledge of me. As he presented the award, he told everyone about me being an EMT, a CPR instructor, etc. He also told of the time that he watched me work with a patient. Which was very surprising to me. It turns out that I responded to a call in the apartment building that Joel lived in. He was on hand as I tended to the patient. I was not aware of who he was at this time ... but he knew who I was. I am truly impressed by his knowledge of the current happenings of the community and of the EMS responders.

"As a funny side note to this. On that day in May 2011, Joel was in Calef's country store and was mentioning that he was going to present the EMT of the year award. My wife, who was in the store, heard him telling people about me. She told Joel who she was and he of course brought her to the presentation across the street at the flag poles.

"It's not often that you get to meet people like Joel and the others that started EMS in Barrington and who placed others before themselves. These people made the effort and sacrifices to create the EMS that Barrington has today."

The general store as a hub for medical services, it turns out, was nothing new. Joel says, "I found an old book on a country store and discovered that two days a week they'd have a doctor come in and see patients. I never knew that. I said, Oh my God. Where I'm an EMT quite a few would come in here and I would take their blood pressure and everything. We went in the office. Had to have it kinda private. If somebody got hurt, they knew that I was an EMT, and they would come and I'd try to take care of it."

Naturally the clerks kidded him. They called him Doc. Doc Sherburne got quite a reputation around town for fixing people up when they needed help quick.

One day, he says, two loggers came by. They'd been working in the woods and one had chewed up his hand with a chainsaw. They didn't know what to do, but the store was close by, so they rushed in. One said: "We need help. My partner has cut himself quite bad." The clerk said, "Doc Sherburne will take care of him."

Joel says: "He come in and when I looked at him, I said, 'Oh come right back out here.' Course we had a sink out here and a chair. I set him right down in the chair. I said, 'Did you just do this?' He said, 'Yes, about twenty minutes ago.'"

The logger had wrapped the hand with a handkerchief, soaked with blood. "You could ring it right out," Joel says. "So I took it off and I looked him over and checked him over and cleaned him up and I said to him, 'I'm going to do this up for you, but you're going to have to go to the emergency room and have some sutures.' He said, 'All right. OK.'"

The logger asked if he was in danger of losing the use of his finger. "No," Joel said, "I don't think so. The digits are not damaged atall."

Joel says, "Course all of 'em around here saw it. Well, there that's all it took. One almost passed out. I thought I was gonna have to treat her, too. I got him all done up. I said to the driver, 'Now you go right to the hospital. It's stopped bleeding cause I've got a pressure dressing on it. But it's going to start again and he's going to have to have stitches.'"

Seems when the logger got to the hospital and the doctor looked over the injury, he admired the skill with which the bandages had been applied and asked who had done it. The logger says, "Doc Sherburne at Calef's Store in Barrington."

The doctor says, "Doc Sherburne? Well, I never have met him, but I'll tell you right now he did a very good job for you."

The logger asked if he was going to lose the use of his finger. The doctor didn't think he would, just as Joel had predicted. Twenty stitches later, the logger was good to go.

Alberta Calef St. Cyr recalls, "Joel was always making a siren noise. Like there was an ambulance coming. He had a little case that he made up and he'd bring it down to work and if anybody got hurt he would patch 'em up. But he always made a production out of it with the siren and the whole thing."

Joel treated a lot of folks in the back room at Calef's. And not a single lawsuit to show for it. Just gratitude. And fingers that healed to pull the cord on a chainsaw another day.

As Told by Joel

Fishing Out the Hook

Another time a father come in with his son. Little kid. He had a fishhook in his finger. They says, "Take him right out back to Doc Sherburne. He'll take care of you."

So he come out and I said, "Well, I guess you've done something." Course the kid was screeching. So I said to the kid, "Now you calm down. Everything is going to be fine."

He said, "Are you going to hurt me?"

I said, "No, I'm not going to hurt you any more than I can help it."

I said to one of the clerks here. "Go out back and find me a pair of pliers that will cut." So they went out and found some. Course the fishhook went right through his finger. The head of it was sticking out.

The little kid said, "What are you gonna do?"

I said, "I'm going to remove that from your finger."

He said, "How are you going to do that?"

I said, "I'm just going to snip the end off here and while you're looking out that winder I'm going to pull it out and it ain't gonna hurt much atall."

He said, "Are you sure?"

I said, "I'm sure."

I snipped it right off quick. I said, "Look over there. See what your dad is doing. He's all worked up over you." And while he's looking I had it out.

He said, "You've taken it out?"

"Sure," I said. "Come over here to the sink. We gotta wash that up. I don't know but you oughta go to the emergency room and get a tetanus shot.

He said, "My dad will take me."

I said, "Well, I'm gonna put some antibiotic on it and clean it up for ya."

By the time I got it done up, it about stopped bleeding.

Joel helped a lot of people over the years. To hear him tell it, he also took a lot of hair-raising rides in the back of emergency service vehicles. Billy McGowan worked many years for Ernest Pinkham, mortician, who ran an ambulance when needed. "He buried most of Strafford," Billy says cheerfully. Ernest was known for his speedy trips to the hospital in his 1951 Cadillac. "Felt like the tires were gonna burn right off the car. If you didn't make it in time, all you had to do was pull the curtain. We scared 'em to death."

Joel said when the Dover crew came out to Barrington with their ambulance, he'd be in the back of the vehicle attending to the patient and he'd say, "Could you slow down? Could you back off a little bit? I want to get the hospital in one piece and I've got the patient under control back he-ah."

On one occasion, helping out with the Irving Benoit hearse/ambulance service, Joel found himself in the company of a new-to-the-job driver. "All he knew was he had to come and help me. We had to go up to the rest home to pick up the body. Guess it had to go to Edgerly."

The driver says, "I hope you know all about this, I've never done this before."

Joel says, "All right, I'll tell you what you gotta do." Nothing much flustered Joel. He was used to giving instructions. They arrived safely at the rest home, put the body in the bag, loaded the body into the vehicle, and were on their way to Edgerly Funeral Home. Joel says to the new driver, "How you doing?"

The driver says, "Well, I'm doing. But if anybody speaks in the back I'm outta here."

Joel says, "You haven't got to worry atall about the one in back. You gotta worry about the ones that's living and how they act and how they treat you."

As Told by Joel

What You Don't Know Won't Hurt Ya, But It Might Scare the Bejesus Out of Ya

I remember this story about this funeral director and his helper went into this filling station to get gas. And his helper had to go to the restroom.

Well, this hitchhiker come along and he says to the undertaker, he said, "Which way are you going?"

And the undertaker said, "We're going right down this way."

And the hitchhiker said, "Do you mind if I have a ride?"

The undertaker said, "No, but you'll have to ride in the back." He said, "We have a body in there. If it don't bother you, fine."

"Oh," he said, "don't bother me a bit."

So he gets in the back. Course the undertaker is sitting in the passenger side and his helper comes out from the restroom. And gets in the hearse and they start down the road. Well they get about five miles down the road, and course they have a little window that you can slide from out front and out back. The hitchhiker slides the window open. He says, "Hey, you mind if I have a smoke?"

Well I guess they took down about nine or ten guardrails. Went right off the road.

And that was a true story. Yes.

Doc Sherburne happily passed on his knowledge to others in innumerable Red Cross classes. He liked teaching. When somebody came to him and said "Joel, I saved a life today" or "I helped somebody today" using what they learned in one of his classes, that was all the pay he needed—that's what floated his boat, churned his butter, and flushed his toilet, too.

As Told by Joel

Molasses in the Maternity Ward

I taught for the Red Cross for about thirty-five years. Oh I don't know how many students I've had, a mess of students. And it was very rewarding.

I used to do emergency child-birth classes for the Red Cross, I had police, state police, nurses. I said, "Now we're gonna have a practical at the end of this class and you're really gonna have to do child-birth on a mannequin." And I said to 'em, "Now this is required. You have got to do this. You've got to have string in your pocket to tie the umbilical cord off. And you've got have about 2 *ccs* of Calef's Fancy Barbados Molasses."

They said, "2 *ccs* of molasses?"

And I said, "Yes, this is mandatory. You've got to have this when I show you how to do a delivery."

They said, "All right."

The trooper, he went to a doctor at Portsmouth Hospital who done deliveries all the time. And he says to him, "You know, I'm in a Red Cross class for emergency childbirth and he said for our practical exam, he told us we got to bring about 2 *cc*s of Calef's Fancy Barbados Molasses." And he says, "What's it for?"

Doctor says, "Beats the hell out of me. Find out." He says, "I've never heard of it."

So, the night of the exam, oh it's about fifteen or sixteen of 'em. They all come in. And I said to 'em, "Now do you have your string?" And they all said yes. I said, "Do you have your molasses?" And they all took out their little bottle of molasses. I said, "That's great."

Now, I said, "I suppose you want to know what the molasses is for?" And they all said, "Yes." And I said, "When the patient starts crowning, you take a little bit of that molasses on your finger and you rub it right around the opening. And when you do that, the little fella will smell that molasses and he'll want to come out and lick it."

You should have seen the trooper when I said it. They didn't expect that was coming but it come. Just to see the expression on their faces. I loved it. A lot of them, they swore a little bit. The trooper went back and told the doctor. Doctor laughed like the devil.

You've got to keep 'em interested.

At times I was a little witty. But at times you've got to be serious. You're not working with machinery. You're working with people.

I done it about every class I done. It went over good.

Joel's involvement with the ambulance service and the Red Cross led to other projects. The town Christmas tree for example. That became an annual gift from the Barrington Ambulance Service.

The service gave to families in need. Organized parades. Erected the flag pole. "We done a lot of stuff," Joel says.

When called upon to serve his town, Joel was apt to say, "Yes."

When Lester Waterhouse retired as head of the Barrington Historical Society, Joel was his chosen successor. Lester stepped down. Joel stepped up.

Longtime friend, David Ranson says: "If you've never seen Joel chair a meeting, it's so classic. He's got a gavel and he knows how to use it. The rhythmic cadence of the way he runs the meeting, everyone revels in the yankeeness of it. Course he has a Toastmaster background."

"Joel," I ask, "are you a Toastmaster?"

"No," he says, "Proctor Silex."

George Musler died in 2016 at age eighty-seven, a great loss to the community. When folks say to Joel, "You know everything there is to know about Barrington," he modestly defers to George Musler. "He knew Barrington," Joel says. "He was selectman for about fifty years." (Actually it was thirty-six, but who's counting?) Joel says, "He didn't have to have a lawyer sitting beside him at meetings. The selectmen did everything." Implication: the selectmen knew what they were doing. In those days, the position of selectman commanded respect because it was a position to which the most respected and knowledgeable people in town aspired and were elected.

Helen Musler says, "It was a very small town when we came in [the 1960s]. The selectmen used to plow the roads." They knew what they were doing and had the skill and gumption to get it done. Those were the days!

Let's put on a show.

Joel's community service extended beyond the boundaries of Barrington. When the need became clear, Joel—among many civic minded people—volunteered to help with the immense project of restoring another local institution, the Rochester Opera House. Some city officials wanted to get rid of the historic building and replace it with offices. It sits right there in downtown Rochester, after all, had been closed for many years, and had deteriorated almost to the point of no return. But, Joel says, Mayor Harvey Bernier took a stand: "No way! I'm going to fight to get this taken care of, fixed up, so we can open it again."

Joel says: "There was once five halls in the country like we have in Rochester. They could raise the floor or level the floor with a mechanism. It's very unique. The last one left in the country—on the national registry of historic places and everything."

The volunteers held raffles, put on shows, sponsored dances. "We did all kinds of things to make money to try to get the opera house open again. It worked. Finally, we were doing so good that things began to happen."

Eventually, the opera house returned to its former glory as a center for entertainment for the Lilac City and surrounds. Joel continued to volunteer. He traded his white Calef's apron for black pants and a white shirt to usher. Sometimes he sold raffle tickets. Sometimes he worked security for the stars who passed through and lit up the stage. One of them was the singer Patti Page.

As Told by Joel

Patti Page—Down to Earth and Terrific

One I met at the Opera House was Patti Page. She lived upcountry and had a syrup business, maple syrup. When she come to the Opera House she brought syrup with her and I had to lug quite a bit in. She sold it. She sold a load of it. She had the jars and you turned the cap off and she'd sing. Some of her songs were in the cap of the syrup. Course I've still got one she gave me.

Oh, she was a character. I was kinda on security and had to watch out for her and everything. I talked to her in the dressing room quite a while. Then I brought this old *TV Guide* from way back and she was on the cover. I took it out of the envelope and I said, "Patti, will you do me a favor."

She said, "What do you want?"

I said, "Will you sign this *TV Guide*?"

She looked at it, "Oh my God," she says, "you've got that? That's ancient." And she said, "Course I'll sign it." And she signed it.

The nicest lady. And, oh, her voice was wonderful. When she done the "Tennessee Waltz," oh my God. She filled the house.

This lady come to the show, course she knew me. She come to me, and she says, "Joel, I've come all the way from York Beach, Maine." And she says "I've got an album of Patti Page and I would love to have her sign it. Kin you help me?"

I says, "Well, let me see what I can do."

During intermission I said, "Patti, this lady is in the audience" and I called her by name. I said, "She thinks you're terrific! She has an old record album of yours. She would love to get it signed."

Patti Page said, "After the second half of the show is over and people start to leave, you have her come right down front of the stage and I will come out and sign it."

I said, "Will you?"

She said, "Sure I will. Long's I don't have a lot of 'em and overdo it."

I said, "All right."

So I went to the lady and I said, "Will you be ready after the show is over? I'll come get you. Bring your record."

She said, "Is Patti Page gonna sign it for me?"

And I said, "Yes, she's gonna do it."

She hugged me and kissed me. I said, "You don't have to do that, you know. Don't get too overexcited."

So after the show, sure enough, we went down to the stage. Patti come right out and talked to her."

For a man who's lived all his life in a small New Hampshire town, Joel has had a surprising number of close encounters with famous people. He made a point of meeting them at the Rochester Opera House, the Rochester Fair, the Hopkinton Fair, the Big E, and, of course, in Calef's Country Store. When he didn't go to them, they came to him.

Ted Williams of Boston Red Sox fame always stopped by Calef's when he was in the area. Which was often. Alberta Calef St. Cyr said: "He gave baseballs to my kids that he signed. He usually had somebody with him. He had a boxer friend, lived over in Epping—Jack Sharkey. Ted loved Calef's cheese—said it was the best thing to catch fish with. He never was in a hurry. He'd go around and talk to anybody in the store. We had quite a few visits with Ted. One time he brought Johnny Pesky. Johnny Pesky didn't really have much to say. He let Ted hold the spotlight. But we were very excited he came."

Joel in full MC regalia.

Joel remembers Ted well. He remembers everything, seems to me. He says, "I met quite a few entertainers and it was great. I go right up to them. They like it!"

When Grampa Jones took the stage at the Hopkinton Fair, Joel was impressed. "I'll never forget it," he says. "Grampa Jones come out on the stage and he says, 'You know, these pants have stuck with me through thick and thin and I'm not gonna let 'em down now.'"

The famous Irish singer Tommy Makem (who lived in nearby Dover), Arthur Godfrey (and his horse, Goalie), Ken McKenzie, Betty Gribbon ("she was funny"), Kitty Wells and her husband Johnny Wright, country singer Buzz Whittaker, the Shaw Brothers, Country Al Green (a close friend)—these were among the notables Joel met and talked with. "I went to Atlantic City to the Miss America Pageant. Met Bert Parks. That was years ago. It was fabulous. Mother and I went down and had a great time. I had the privilege to meet him afterwards. Great guy. Wonderful to talk to. And he had a great voice. The Convention hall—what a building. Beautiful girls. I had eye strain."

Joel himself has taken to the stage from time to time. At the drop of a hat, he'll don his tuxedo and act as master of ceremonies for fundraisers and variety shows. He performed with Dick Curless, the country singer. "I was part of the show," Joel says. "Comedy. I'd come out and do two or three songs. Like 'Good Night Irene,' but I had my own version

Joel hosts bluegrass musician Cecil Abels and friends under the big top.

or whatever. You might say a little off color, maybe a bright yellow. He thought it was terrific. Then I was with the John Penny Band. We had him at the fair a lot. He wanted me to go on the road with him."

The road to Calef's is one often travelled by politicians and Joel has made friends with many of them. Jeanne Shaheen—now Senator, then Governor—dedicated a proclamation to Joel. "For being here so long," Joel says. "I think it was fifty years." Former governor Craig Benson stopped by. As did President Jimmy Carter and his son Chip.

At one time quite a lot of Calef's cheese went to Washington, D.C., for various functions. Calef's fan Senator Tom McIntyre would order whole wheels. A little taste of New Hampshire for the big wigs.

Joel has met Maggie Hassan—now Senator, then Governor— "eight or nine times."

"Did you give her any advice?" I asked.

"Well, no. She didn't ask for any. I probably could have."

Joel describes all the entertainers and sports figures and most of the politicians, as "down to earth" and "terrific!" My theory: Joel brings out the best qualities in just about everybody he meets. He just can't help it!

≋ Chapter 6 ≋

Cuttin' the Cheese

J oel Sherburne should, probably, hold the Guinness World Record for cutting the most cheese of any living person (or dead for that matter). If Guinness had a cheese cutting category. Which they don't. We know this because a few years back Lindy Horton nominated him for the honor, but Guinness didn't bite.

Calef's cheese is cut and wrapped by hand. Nothing automated. Just Joel and his wire cheese cutter.

Joel at work. That forty-pound wheel of cheese has met its match.

Action shot.

"Do you suppose you've cut a million pounds of cheese?" I ask.

"It don't have to be right on," he says. "But approximately. Maybe I don't want to know. Tons. I've cut tons. Cut it, wrap it, price it and everything."

I say, "We could figure it out. With math."

Joel says, "Like today I probably cut about seventy pounds. Tomorrow I'm going to have to cut more Rat Trap, and they go like thirty-five-, forty-pound wheels. I'll probably do two of them tomorrow. Plus the flavored cheddars."

"Would it be fair to say about a hundred pounds a day on average?"

"Yuh. On weekends I do more. September 7 it's gonna start my 59th year. In 2017—I'll be starting sixty. I work seven days a week. I come to work every morning at 5:00 or so. Course I'm off at 11:00. Way back, we used to be open Friday and Saturday nights until 9:00. I say to people, I like to come to work. I enjoy it. And the team I work with is excellent. People say, 'You are sick.' I say, 'Well that could be a possibility.'"

So let's do some math with allowances for time off. Nobody, not even Joel Sherburne, works seven days a week for sixty years. He took trips to Nashville and Atlantic City and other excitin' places. He also took the very occasional sick day. And, truth be told, there were times when he landed in the hospital for ailments that set him back a week. As Joel says, "That's normal."

Variations in the length of Joel's work day must also be taken into account. When he started he was still in high school, so he worked after school until closing time, and had not yet received his training in the cuttin' of the cheese. Later he worked full time and beyond, as the head cheese man. Now he works six-hour days. Of course, during that time, he cuts all the cheese he thinks will be needed for the full day. Conservatively, even if we say he cut cheese 6 days a week (which is low) X 48 weeks (4 weeks off for vacation or sick time—which seems excessive) X 50 years (accounting for a generous 10 years of stocking, bagging, clerking, and cutting cheese only part time) X an average of 100 pounds/day. That equals (drumroll): 1,440,000.

Yuh, Joel, you've cut a million pounds of cheese and then some, easy.

A lot of people, customers and colleagues alike, fondly recall Joel's imaginary board, which served as a handy and necessary accessory for busy cheese days. And at Calef's, almost every day is busy in the cheese department. People must have their cheese. They demand it. Lines form.

Snappy Old Cheese
stands the test of time.

Joel must work fast. So to facilitate the process his imaginary board translated vague requests for amounts of cheese into pounds. When the line got long and the cheese was flying out the door one pound after another, he just didn't have time to ask customers what they meant by a little bit, a slice, a chunk, a hunk, a wedge, a sliver, or a piece.

"I'd cut steady on a Sunday afternoon," Joel said. "No let up. That's why I kinda come up with an invisible list." The customers would say what they wanted. Joel would consult his invisible list on his imaginary board and cut accordingly. "A piece was maybe three-quarters of a pound. A chunk was about a pound and a quarter," he said. "They never objected. One would say she'd like a slice, so I'd slice it right off and give it to her," explaining that according to his chart, "That's a slice. You got it? I just couldn't mess around. There was a steady line. I cut all afternoon. It was so excitin'! I had a cutter with a wire. Couldn't mess around with a knife. We'd still be there. They loved it."

As Told by Joel

How Much Cheese Did You Say?

One day this lady came in and she says to me, "I would like about three quarters of a pound of cheddar."

So I said all right. I cut it and put it on the scale.

She looked at it and she said, "I don't think I want that. Could you cut me about a half a pound?"

I said, "Yes, I kin." So I cut a half a pound.

And she says, "You know that is still too much." She says, "Can you possibly cut me a quarter of a pound?"

And I says, "Yes, I will do it." So I cut that and put it on the scale.

She says, "Well, that's too small."

So I says to her, I says, "Lady, I've cut three pieces of cheese here. And you don't want any of 'em."

I says, "I'm going to cut one more and you bettah want it, cause I don't think you really know what you want."

So guess what, she took the first one I cut. Yes.

Ninety-five percent are great customers. But sometimes you get one—it ruins the day. Throws you right off kiltah.

I almost said, "Are you from Salem? Do you have a broom?"

I finally said to her, "This is it. Ain't cuttin' no more!"

In the Calef's archives (a cardboard box of photos and clippings) I discovered a typed manuscript by Herb Howe—two yellowing pages with the catchy title "A Country Store Goes National on a Single Item Without Losing the Quaint Qualities of Rustic Service and Atmosphere." The article is undated, but it is set during the time brothers Harlan and Clarence ran the store and after their father, Austin, had died. The article mentions sending cheese to service men in the European and Pacific theatres, so it's definitely World War II era.

Where or if the article was ever published is unclear. It's in draft form with handwritten corrections. I'm guessing Howe ran it by one of the brothers for accuracy and that the brother did a little editing. For example, Howe wrote that at Calef's, "Some local yokel might engage you in conversation to point out that the nearby intersecting highway used to be a railroad." The handwritten note crosses out "local yokel" and substitutes "neighbor," with the tart comment "No yokels around here."

It's a terrific article, as Joel would say—a snapshot of Calef's business practices that is detailed, colorful, and of its time. Howe attributes much of the store's success to its cheese, which, he asserts, sells itself with minimal advertising, maybe $30 a year according to store records. And that $30 includes painting the roadside signs and printing the wrapping papers and labels.

He writes, "The East Barrington post office serves less than 200 families but it handles 50 tons of Calef cheese year after year." Fifty tons! In the 1940s. And that cheese went all over the country and overseas, too. People couldn't get enough of it. Still can't. Howe explains that

Austin Calef "discovered a secret and kept quiet about it." He calls this a strange but strangely effective marketing technique. "He and his two sons let the secret do its own promoting through word-of-mouth discussion of the product's merits." In other words, the Calefs discovered a method for making their cheese especially tasty and refused to reveal their secret to anyone. Which got people talking about both the cheese and the mystery of its production. Which made people want that special cheese even more.

But wait. Calef's famous cheese is not, technically, made in New Hampshire, never was and still isn't. In the 1940s, the brothers imported it from Herkimer County, New York. The secret discovered by Austin, protected by his sons and grandsons (and still a secret today) lies in the aging—something about the aging. At least that's what Howe believed. He writes: "The senior Calef found out many years ago that the moist cellars beneath his store were ideal for ripening cheddar cheese. Something in the soil evidently did the trick. He experimented with one-year aging, then two-year and finally three-year ripening. Three years' storage produced the kind of cheese customers wanted but seldom found. When the three-year cheese reaches the consumer in Seattle or Sarasota and the multiple wrappings are removed it will be found wringing wet with moisture. And crumbly. And bitey."

As Told by Joel

How Snappy Old Cheese Got Its Name

One day some fishermen come in here and they wanted some very strong cheddar.

Austin says, "I just come from down cellar and I found a beauty." He says, "It's the sharp."

He gave them a sample. And they said, "Oh my God. That is snappy!" So Austin got the idea of Snappy Old Cheese. Every bite tastes right.

And we've always used it. That was before I was here, so more than sixty years ago. Probably over a hundred years.

We still keep a few wheels of cheese down cellar. But we have a warehouse now for the aging. Course the aging process is kind of a secret. It's been in the Calef family and never let out. And I still continue that. I don't tell 'em. It's a secret. It's the aging process that makes it very unique. My lips are sealed. Just like Elmer's glue. Sealed.

Joel loves cheese, the sharper the better. "Makes you sit right up and take notice," he says. "We ship it all over. It's the staple of the store. It's always been very famous. People, once they try it, they keep coming back."

Roger and Harlan, he recalls, made regular truck runs to Boston to pick up the cheese wheels in firkins. The brothers would be gone all day and would bring home anywhere from 250 to about four hundred pounds. They alternated the cheese runs with general runs to the city to stock up on groceries.

When the big loads of cheese arrived, they'd have to be moved down cellar to begin the aging process. The wheels weighed about forty pounds each. Workers would slide them down a wide board through the bulkhead. Then they had to be stacked. It was a labor-intensive operation.

During the aging process, every three or four months, a chisel-like device, known as a cheese iron, would be inserted into the round to pull out a sample. "They'd taste it," Joel says, "to see how good it was coming. They would test them, try 'em. Then they a-course had another special process that we don't talk about."

Because it's a secret! "Let 'em think about it," he says. "Good for some of 'em."

I tried my darnedest to get Joel to reveal that special process, but his lips were sealed, like Elmer's glue.

Artist Jake Rheume's rendition of our cheese man at work.

As Told by Dan Waterhouse

When my brothers were working here they stored the cheese down cellar, so the challenge was who could carry the most rounds up the stairs.

So this kid carried five.

My brother he grabbed six and got part way up the stairs and got caught by Harlan.

"What are you doin?" Harlan said. "You're gonna break them stairs because they can't take that much weight."

Not, "You're gonna get hurt," but "You're gonna break them stairs." That was from Harlan.

Joelism —"Jocko." When you have something of particular importance to say, instead of calling a person by his name, you grab his attention by calling him Jocko. As in: "Stop fooling around with those cheese rounds on the stairs, Jocko, before they break and you and the cheese go ass over tea kettle."

The Rat Trap Cheddar wins the prize as Calef's current best seller. It's hand packed and extra creamy. The older the cheese, the bitier. Joel says, "Some we just got in. Eight years old. Oh lord, that'll set you back a week. Oh yuh. You ain't kiddin. It makes a man set up and take notice."

Calef's carries a wider variety of cheeses now than it used to. "Way back," Joel says, "all we had was just the basic cheddars. Now we've got all the flavored ones like roasted garlic and steak house onion, maple bacon. Oh my God, you name it we've got it."

No more trips to Boson, the wheels are delivered from a number of different producers. Though a few still age in the magic cellar, most await their perfectly aged debut in the warehouse.

Some old friends of Joel and Calef's got to talking about how strong the strongest of the cheese really was. Did it make your hair stand on end? Your eyeballs bulge out of your head? Did it shrivel your tongue? Cling to the roof of your mouth? Make you cry tears of gastronomic ecstasy?

Dan Waterhouse recalled some customers from Massachusetts who made the mistake of saying they wanted a large quantity of really sharp cheese. Calef's takes such a request seriously. Turns out there was a wheel in the cellar that had been "sitting around forever and a day. It was one of the rounds in the back area and they forgot about it." Somebody dug it out. And the people from Massachusetts thought it was just the ticket, the bitiest of the bitey.

The clerks wrapped that round of cheese five or six times. Placed it in the trunk of the car. And away those Massachusetts folks went, happy as quahogs.

"They got down below Lee somewhere, and they turned that car right around," Dan said. "They came right back to the store and said, 'Hey can you ship this to us, cause we can't stand sitting in the car with it?' It smelled so bad. They had it in the trunk with the windows down and they still couldn't do it."

Now that's a testimonial to a really sharp cheese—Calef's bread and butter (so to speak) for over a hundred years.

The Story of
Calef's Cheddar...

We hope you enjoy your Snappy Old Cheese. We have been aging our cheddar for the past 148 years. These exceptional cheddars deserve special treatment to provide you with the best cheddar flavor experience.

Please refrigerate immediately.

Once opened, rewrap your cheese tightly in plastic wrap and store in the refrigerator.

Cheese is a live product. If surface mold develops, simply cut it off and rewrap in fresh plastic wrap. The flavor and the quality will not be affected.

Wrapped and stored, your cheese will keep for many months making freezing unnecessary.

Storage at warm temperatures may cause our cheddar to "whey off." This condition occurs when butterfat separates from the cheese and may affect the appearance and aroma. The flavor will not be affected.

When serving Snappy Old Cheese, please allow the cheese to come to room temperature. The flavor, texture and aroma will be richer and more fully developed. We guarantee you will be pleased with our cheddars. Please feel free to contact us with any questions, comments or to share a favorite recipe! And do stop by when you are in the neighborhood.

Cheddar Facts

- The name "Cheddar" is taken from a small town in England where cheese of this type was first produced over four hundred years ago
- It takes over ten gallons of milk to make one pound of Cheddar
- An average Holstein cow produces six gallons of milk per day
- Our Cheddar tastes best if served at room temperature but will store well in your refrigerator for months if tightly wrapped
- Mold may develop on the surface but will not penetrate the cheese or spoil it, simply cut of the molded area and enjoy the rest
- Freezing will not affect the flavor but it will alter the texture and consistency significantly. Store wrapped tightly in the refrigerator

All of our Cheese is "Snappy Old Cheddar," a term used by the Calef's for many generations to describe our delicious cheese!

Country Store Cheddars

- Rat Trap – Old Country Store hand packed 40-lb. wheels; creamy, rich flavor, our most popular cheese
- Sharp – In spite of its name our least sharp cheese, mellow creamy flavor
- Extra Sharp – A hint of that sharp bite with a deep creamy texture
- Super Sharp – Starting to get sharp now, still a creamy texture with robust flavor

Aged Cheddars

- 4 Year Aged – Crumbly texture with crystals starting to form, delicious
- 5 Year Aged – Strong sharp flavor, crystalized and very crumbly
- 6 Year Aged – Very Strong sharp flavor, crystalized and very crumbly

- Wicked Sharp – Getting serious now, with a sharp bite and a bit of crumble, not for the faint of heart
- Flavored Cheddars – Start with mild creamy cheddar and add natural flavors, wonderful, Maple Bacon, Steakhouse Onion, Roasted garlic to name a few
- Smokey – Sharp Cheddar hand smoked in the store using Joel's famous recipe

Cheddar Pumpkin Dip

Ingredients

- Non-stick cooking spray
- 1 can cannellini beans, drained and rinsed
- 1 ½ cups pumpkin puree (fresh pumpkin roasted is tastier, canned is easier)
- 1 clove garlic, minced
- Salt and pepper, to taste
- 6 ounces Calef's Buffalo Wing Cheddar, shredded (about 1 ½ cups)
- Sundried tomatoes, roma tomatoes and/or green onions, for garnish
- Tortilla chips, carrot sticks and celery sticks, for dipping

Directions

1. Preheat oven to 350°F. Spray six ramekins with non-stick cooking spray.
2. Combine cannellini beans, pumpkin, garlic, salt and pepper in food processor and puree until smooth.
3. Divide mixture between the six ramekins. Sprinkle the cheese on top of the bean and pumpkin mixture and stir to incorporate the cheese throughout. Sprinkle top with diced sundried tomatoes, if using.
4. Bake for 15 minutes or until bubbling and heated throughout.
5. Garnish with tomatoes and/or green onion, if using. Serve with chips and veggies to dip.

≋ Chapter 7 ≋

Beyond the Cheese

A nd so goes the story of the little town of Barrington and Calef's Store, told mostly through the eyes of Joel Sherburne, the honorary mayor of Barrington and Calef's most loyal, longest serving, and (it appears to me) most beloved employee.

Customers think Joel is a member of the Calef's family—I've seen it. At the annual Christmas soiree, so well attended that there's hardly any "room for the feet," one man bought a postcard of the store and asked Joel to sign it. He said it would be great to have an actual Calef sign the card. Kinda historic. Joel didn't quibble. He just signed it. The man didn't seem to know the difference. Or care.

Joel is as much a part of Calef's Country Store as the phone on the wall, the loading dock out back, or the magical soil in the cellar. He is as much a part of Calef's and the tradition of the small-town general store as the stories that hold our memories of how things used to be, and how they still are—at least for a few minutes when you walk through the door and take in the sights, smells, sounds. As Joel says, "You smile all over your face." Nostalgia warms you like aroma of the fresh-made coffee and cider doughnuts, the tang of pepper jelly on a cracker, the old wood stove that Jack Bodge got going every chill morning to help his friend Alberta after his friend Roger died.

That stove works just as well as it always did. The values of neighborliness, service, hard work, honesty, and good humor live on.

Leola J. Pepler wrote a poem about Calef's Country store for *NH Profiles Magazine* in 1940s, near as I can figure based on the content. I've been unable to find the actual issue. *Profiles* has been out of business for decades. And Leola is not on Facebook. But somebody thought enough of the poem to save it all these years. Hope it floats your boat.

The Ballad of Calef's Country Store

On Barrington Road, not far from Dover,
You could hunt the whole world over
To find the equal of Calef's Store,
With all its food and gimmicks galore.
Here is a sugar barrel close by the cheese
And fresh ground pepper, to make you sneeze.
Right near the pickle barrel, lots of crackers;
This combination has plenty of backers.
Thick, dark molasses, sold in bulk:
Children who taste it will never sulk.
Home-made doughnuts, each with a hole,
Taste mighty good, as over you stroll
On to the counter where they sell meat
That is cut and trimmed, ever so neat
If you need a new mower to cut the grass
You may find one draped with fresh "sass."
Now this is not all you will find in the store;
Just hold your patience, there is always more.
There are dresses and smocks and blue dungarees,
To fit the young miss as tight as you please.
Or, if you desire a villain to nip,
Why not buy a long buggy whip?
Watch for red onions, hung on a string,

These are good for any old thing.
And dark smoked herring is a tasty bit
That cooked in cream will make a hit.
If for ginger snaps you have a yen,
Order some by word or pen.
Whether it's shoes or a catty nap,
Come to Calef's, you won't need a map.
They have fresh eggs equipped with a cackle.
They even sell good fishing tackle.
They sell a hundred loaves in a single day,
Of homemade bread, and that ain't "hay."
A homemade turnover in fresh pineapple
Will liven up Philadelphia scapple.
On the Barrington Road, not far from Dover,
You will find it pays to be a rover;
For once you find Calef's store,
There you'll trade for evermore.

Cheesy Cheddar Stuffed Meatballs

Ingredients

Meatballs:

- 1 ¼ pounds ground beef
- ½ onion, finely chopped
- 1 inch piece of ginger, finely chopped
- 2 cloves garlic, finely chopped
- ¼ teaspoon salt
- ½ teaspoon pepper
- 1 teaspoon turmeric
- 1 teaspoon paprika
- 2 teaspoons chopped cilantro
- 2 ounces Calef's Rat Trap Cheddar, grated (about ½ cup)
- 1 egg
- Calef's Aged Cheddar, cut into cubes

Spicy Cheese Dipping Sauce:

- ½ cup milk
- 3 ounces Calef's Rat Trap Cheddar, grated (about ¾ cup)
- ¼ teaspoon chili powder
- ¼ teaspoon paprika

Directions

Meatballs:

1. Preheat oven to 375°F.
2. Mix all the ingredients together, except for the cubed cheddar.
3. Mix into a ball, enclosing a cube of cheddar in the middle.
4. Bake at 375°F for 30 minutes.

Spicy Cheese Dipping Sauce:

1. Place milk, cheese, chili powder and paprika in a saucepan over medium heat for about 10 minutes. Stir frequently so cheese melts evenly.
2. Serve with meatballs.

≋ Chapter 8 ≋

A Few Other Remarkable New England Country Stores Well Worth the Trip

Brown and Hopkins Country Store

Chepachet, Rhode Island

Not too big, not too small, Brown and Hopkins (brownandhopkins.com) in Chepachet, Rhode Island, charms customers with its worn floors, beamed ceilings, and potbellied stove. It stocks the usual—penny candy, historical prints, braided rugs, Vermont cheddar (does Rhode Island have no cows?), yard goods, and even antiques. Chepachet itself is a destination for antique hounds.

It claims to be the oldest continuously running country store in the country. (So does the Brick Store in Bath, New Hampshire, and probably a few others.) The building was erected in 1799 and used as a hattery. In 1807, Ira Evans turned it into a general store and that's what it's been ever since. Several owners have run the business over the years, most recently Elizabeth Yuill of Foster, Rhode Island.

In 2014, paranormal investigators (creepyplaces.webs.com) took stock of a ghostly presence named Ella or maybe Beatrice. The half-hour video can be viewed on the Brown and Hopkins website. It is creepy indeed to see the wires of the dowsing rods cross when the investigators ask the ghost (they're pretty sure it's a young woman) to make her presence known. She doesn't answer questions directly, but seems to like penny candy and the company of customers. She gets a little frustrated at being invisible and unable to communicate easily. It's no fun being ignored for a hundred fifty years.

Her frustration shows in the little tricks she plays, like braiding the scarfs hanging from the wire mannequin or making monkey chains out of *S* hooks.

The coffee is always hot at Brown and Hopkins, with proceeds supporting local charities. So whether you're looking for good coffee, a mug to drink it in, or the feeling of the hair rising on the back of your neck as you climb the stairs to the haunted (or is it?) bedroom, Brown and Hopkins Country Store is worth the trip. If you dare!

Fadden's General Store and Maple Sugarhouse

North Woodstock, New Hampshire

Just about all New England country stores sell maple syrup, but Fadden's makes their own. Used to be the Fadden family collected maple sap in buckets with wooden spiles. That was way back when the store was founded in 1896. Now there's so much demand for their award-winning syrup, they've upgraded to stainless steel and food-grade plastic, with seventeen miles (give or take) of hose, and 7,500 taps (give or take) for the production of about 2,500 gallons of syrup annually.

It's real fine syrup, garnering lots of blue ribbons at fairs and regional honors. One year it won the Governor's Cup for the best maple syrup in North America. So this crop of Faddens, now running the show, have good reason to say customers will "experience seven generations of maple perfection."

On Main Street at the general store, a rambling yellow house with a distinctive striped awning, you'll find all things maple, as well as general fare for tourists and locals. Well worth the trip, especially during boiling season when you can tour the boiling operation and see for yourself how the clear sap of the sugar maple turns into liquid gold, or, more precisely, shades of amber. Find out more at nhmaplesyrup.com.

Harmon's Cheese and Country Store

Sugar Hill, New Hampshire

Many country stores, like Calef's, do as much business on-line as in store. Harmon supports its on-line business with a colorful, informative web site (harmonscheese.com) that paints a vivid picture of the ambiance of the store and beauty of the area. Sugar Hill is one of the most beautiful towns in New Hampshire. Yuh, it's on the beautiful towns list. And why not, set up high, lots of woods, open fields, stone walls, mountain views. It even has a covered bridge spanning the Ammonoosuc. Now that's not only beautiful, it's picturesque.

A visit is well worth the drive, especially during the Lupine Festival, with special events scheduled over three weeks in the spring. Harmon's sits smack dab in the middle of scenic Sugar Hill, at the center of activity for the festival.

Owner Maxine Aldrich writes that it all began "in 1954, when John and Kate Harmon retired from life in New York City and followed their dream to own a country store to quaint Sugar Hill, New Hampshire. Soon after, John and Kate were presented with a unique opportunity—to start a mail order business. In 1955, a salesman told John that his firm had discovered some cheese that had been 'forgotten' for two years. John recognized the potential of selling 'aged' cheese and purchased all of it, about a half ton, at 54¢ a pound. John used his advertising expertise to start a mail-order business with that half-ton of cheese. Word of the magnificent flavor of Harmon's aged cheese began to spread, and soon customers began calling it the 'World's Greatest' Cheddar Cheese.'"

Harmon's also features chocolate, mustard, pickles, sweatshirts (Patriots and Red Sox), meats, crackers, cookies, and the Lupine Festival Cookbook. And that's just for starters.

Joelism —"Heifer Dust." As in: "If I say I make the best cheese in the world and you say you make the best cheese in the world, one of us is full of heifer dust."

Hussey's General Store

Windsor, Maine

Holy mackerel, Hussey's General Store is a big 'un. It claims the title "Largest General Store in Maine." Yankee Magazine readers voted it "Best One-Stop Shopping in New England." Eat your heart out, Walmart.

Check out their detailed website, husseygeneralstore.com, for a surprising variety of goods. In one photograph their roadside sign advertises: Guns, Wedding Gowns, Cold Beer.

According to the website: "Harland Hussey opened his grocery business in October 1923, when he remodeled an old stable. He also stocked some men's wearing apparel. His son, Elwin, was born the same year Harland opened the business. He recalls the 'good old days' when obtaining merchandise was a problem. 'Of the two I prefer the new days,' Hussey says, 'if only for the transportation.'"

The goods are laid out in departments—large departments. You need fishing tackle (bobbers, lures, trolling motors, bug nets), that'll be in Outdoors.

Got chickens, goats, chickens, pigs? You'll find plenty of feed in the Grain Department. All country stores, including Calef's, used to stock grain; not so much anymore.

Doing some building? You can pick up a few bags of cement. Outhouse getting pungent? Hussey's carries hydrated lime to tamp the smell right down. Still feeling energetic? Stock up on painting, plumbing, and gardening supplies.

Need a new outfit. Hussey's carries Carhartt duds for the whole family, along with other name brands like Dickies and Wigwam.

If you make the trip, plan to make a day of it. Perk up with a snack or a meal from the deli or one of the daily specials—soups, salads, sandwiches, and pizza. Top it off with a Wicked Whoopie Pie and you'll know you've been somewhere.

Joelism —"Got to." As in: "When the pile get's high in the outhouse and the odor starts to waft, discourage it with add a few cups of lime. Got to."

Old Country Store and Emporium

Mansfield, Massachusetts

This twelve-room journey back in time is "tucked away," according to visitingnewengland.com, in the "tranquil neighborhood of Old Mansfield Village." Set your GPS for 26 Otis Street, West Mansfield, Massachusetts, and you might soon be tucking into homemade jams, jellies, or peanut butter (from a peanut butter machine) on a cracker, topped off with a pickle that was actually pickled in a barrel on the premises. Meanwhile listen to the clingy clangy notes of "By the Light on the Silvery Moon" played on the nickelodeon.

The Old Country Store and Emporium specializes in classics—classic games and classic toys. The kind you played with as a kid. Or your Mom did. Or your Grampa. It offers furnishings and decorations from lighting to rugs. Seventeen hundred feet of floor space allows room for big items like grandfather clocks, as well small items like homemade fudge.

Shopkeepers Chris and Lauryn Baker "cordially invite you to share a rare and wonderful experience." Their store (oldcountrystoreonline.com) "has been a purveyor of old tyme provisions, oddments, fancies, decorations, house wares and elegant gifts for over 180 years. Heck, Andrew Jackson, the 7th President of the United States, was in the White House when our doors first opened!" Heck, this store is so old it could be called olde. They're not just purveyors of "old tyme" provisions, they're also "Purveyors of American Values since 1829."

Drive careful on those busy Massachusetts highways. Some of them have four lanes, one way! Yikes.

Joelism —"Oh plutz." As in: "Oh plutz, I'm in the far-left lane and there's two lanes full of Massachusetts drivers between me and the exit to Mansfield. Don't know as I'm gonna make it."

Vermont Country Store

Weston and Rockingham, Vermont

Actually, it's Vermont Country Store*s*, one on Main Street in Weston, which opened in 1946, and the newer store in Rockingham. The business started as a catalogue sent out by Vrest and Mildred Orton to a mailing list of 1000 people, mostly folks on their Christmas card list. Their vision: provide things that were "practical, useful, and actually work," which evolved into "Purveyors of the Practical and Hard-to-Find."

Vrest writes that he was inspired by his father's general store in North Calais, Vermont, "where most of the men came in the evenings to wait for the horse-drawn stage that brought the mail from Montpelier, thirteen miles away.... The store was warm and cozy. It smelled of harness, coffee, smoky kerosene lamps, tobacco, and sugar maple wood burning in the big stove."

This was in the 60s, the 1860s that is.

The stores remain in the family. Lyman Orton and his sons Cabot, Gardner and Eliot represent the fourth and fifth generations of storekeepers.

The Vermont Country Store Catalogue is full of enticing wares, but nothing beats a visit to the stores themselves. Last visit, I bought a red flannel dress that I plan to wear on Christmas for the rest of my life. It's got black velour trim! Some fancy. I got it on sale on the second floor of the Rockingham store where the bargains hide. I also bought a wind-up tin duck with a whirly-gig hat riding a tricycle. Had to have it.

Yup, they sell high quality clothes—country style—for men, women, and kids. They sell lots of handy stuff for the kitchen including oilcloth table coverings. In my family, growing up, every table had one. They are well stocked with supplies for personal health, hygiene, and beauty. And of course, they're famous for their eats—including Vermont cheese and Vermont maple syrup. Plus candy. Remember the old-fashioned ribbon candy that looked so pretty in the box—they got it.

For the full range of goods, visit their website vermontcountrystore.com. Or better yet, stop by. May I recommend Vermont during foliage season?

More Beloved Country Stores

I polled my friends and acquaintances (yup, Facebook) for their favorite country stores. Patterns emerged. A person's favorite country store is the one he or she patronized as a child. Or the one closest to home. Or the one in the town where Gramma and Grampa lived. Or the one on the way to the mountains, a pit stop on the annual family trip. People have personal connections to their favorites. Good memories. Good experiences. We love our country stores. And, no surprise, we miss them when they're gone.

In my unscientific poll, Calef's garnered a lot of votes. So did the Vermont Country Store, Harmon's in Sugar Hill, and Zeb's in downtown Conway. The Brick Store in Bath (aforementioned contender for longest running) got several enthusiastic nods.

Cheryl Bacon Nolan recommends the Gorham Corner Market in Gorham, NH. She appreciates the focus on local products—fresh eggs, homemade breads, goat milk and soaps and lotions, locally crafted hats and grocery bags, "and lots, lots more." The Gorham Corner Market, under new management, she says "is just blooming."

Andy Robertson noted that Young's in Pittsburg is one of the few general stores in New Hampshire that's also a liquor store. (I didn't know that was even legal—but they do things different in the North Country.) They also grind their own hamburger.

So does Danis Market in Pittsfield—more of a grocery store than a general store but with a lot of local flavor. One patron said, "They even rang my seltzer as tonic. Don't see that every day." Tonic—for those of you not from around here—is the New England term for carbonated beverages, like Moxie—a soft drink found only in New England (pretty sure) and mostly at country stores.

Someone suggested Dick's Guns, Guitars and Groceries, be included in this list because the name covers a lot of country, even though it's in Churubusco, New York.

Other stores deemed worthy of special recognition by poll participants (located in New Hampshire unless otherwise noted):

Alley's General Store, Martha's Vineyard, MA—You guessed it, "the oldest store on Martha's Vineyard." No website as of this printing, but they are found on Facebook.

Black's Gift and Paper Shop, Wolfeboro—Wolfeboro on Lake Winnipesaukee is famous for being "the oldest summer resort in America." <http://www.blacksgiftsnh.com/>

Cardigan Country Store, 231 Lake St, Bristol, NH. <http://www.cardiganmtnorchard.com/>

The Cheese Shop at the Calvin Coolidge Historic Site, Plymouth Notch, VT—Offering tastings, tours and a heaping helping of history. <http://www.plymouthartisancheese.com/> (A great online resource is the website for the Vermont Association of Independent Country Stores: <http://vaics.org/stores>.)

Chichester Country Store—Carries, some say, the best cider doughnuts in the state of New Hampshire. <http://www.milessmithfarm.com/chichester-country-store.html>

Currier's Quality Market, Glover, VT. <http://centerofthekingdom.com/food/curriers-quality-market>

Dakin Farm, Ferrisburgh, VT—Specializing in "pure Vermont specialty food." <http://www.dakinfarm.com/>

Dan and Whit's, Norwich, VT. <http://www.danandwhitsonline.com/>

Danbury Country Store—next door to Dick's Village Store. For some reason this little town has (almost) always had two country stores, side by side. <http://danburycountrystore.com/>

Demmons Store, 368 Stage Road, West Nottingham, NH—Kevin Foster says, "When we first came into disposable income we used to ride our bikes down the road to buy penny candy there." Neighbor Adi Rule says: "Us too! We'd buy chilled candy bars from the freezer." Demmons is about as country as you can get.

Dick's Village Store—Next to the Danbury Country Store, across the road from the infamous Hippie Hill—look it up. Check out their Facebook page.

Dodge's Store, 7 Central Square, New Boston, NH.

Jeannotte's Market, Nashua—A favorite of Adelle Leiblein and many others. It qualifies as a country store because, Adelle says, it "sells baked beans on Saturday, handmade caramels for church fundraisers, and French gorton, meats sourced from Canada." She says, "I believe they grind their own beef (80/20 of course), subs to order, their own ham salad, ditto chicken salad with walnuts and cranberries (so fancy)." You "used to be able to get Moxie there, don't know about now. Course now they sell lottery tickets, so some things old school have been lost. Very friendly, help to your car with big bundles for old folks like me!" Check them out on Facebook.

SIXTY YEARS OF CUTTIN' THE CHEESE

J Town Deli, Jackson—excellent takeout from sausage to cupcakes. "Come and be happy." <http://jtowndeli.com/>

Liar's Paradise Pizza and Store in Nottingham—At Liar's, as the locals call it, according to Alden Dill, "You usually still find a group of guys drinkin' coffee and bitchin' about the weather in the corner." <http://www.liarsparadise.com/>

Lindy's Country Store, 405 Middle Rd, Brentwood, NH 03833— "Still looks like most used to. And if you cross the street, you can check out Crowley Falls."

Lyme Country Store, Lyme. <http://www.lymecountrystore.com/>

Mae's Store, Plainfield, VT—Steve Bumgarner laments: "Actually it probably doesn't exist any longer but in the mid 70's (1970s that is) it was the place to be." In his recollection, "Mae ran the store in her bathrobe, but maybe it was a muumuu." (Or, as they say in Vermont, a moomoo.)

Moulton's Market, Amherst. <http://www.moultonsmarket.com/>

Newfields Country Store, Newfields. <http://www.newfieldscountrystore.com/>

Old Country Store and Museum, Moultonborough. < http://nhcountrystore.com/>

Old Wethersfield Country Store, Wethersfield, CT. <http://www.owcsct.com/>

The Other Store, Tamworth—The name itself is an example of dry Yankee humor. Check out their Facebook page.

Petersham Country Store, Petersham, MA—"A classic."
<http://petershamstore.com/>

Reney's, Grantham. Fondly remembered by Andy Davis as "the general store from my childhood, back when Grantham was Grantham. Like so many, it's no longer with us."

Ripton General Store, Route 125, Ripton, VT.
<http://vaics.org/stores?store=38>

Robie's Country Store—By the railroad bridge over the Merrimack in Hooksett.
<https://en.wikipedia.org/wiki/Robie's_Country_Store>

Sullivan's Little Country Store, Sullivan—The homemade doughnuts are legendary. See their Facebook page.

Tamworth Lyceum, Tamworth. <http://tamworthlyceum.com/>

Vernondale General Store, North Sutton—Papa Joe Gaudet says: "It's got penny candy and a soda bah. Tell Bob I sent you ovah for some cheese. He's a good cuttah too."
<https://www.vernondalestore.com/>

The Warren Store, Warren, VT—Listed as one of the five best Vermont Country Stores by *Yankee Magazine*. "We have a little something for everyone."
<https://www.warrenstore.com/>

Washington General Store, 29 N Main St, Washington, NH —
According to Brady Carlson, author of *Dead Presidents*, locals
sometimes recite original poems to presidential candidates. New
Hampshire gets a lot of candidates passing through during presidential primary season. Luckily it's not an annual event. Every
four years is about all we can take. Check out their Facebook page.

Wayside Country Store, Marlborough, MA.
<http://www.waysidecountrystore.com/>

Ye Olde Sale Shoppe, Effingham— In business since 1972. "The little
shoppe with the big heart." <http://www.yeoldesaleshoppe.com/>

Next stop Barrington, home to Calef's famous country store. If we don't have it, you don't
need it.

Resources

Boston Globe, "Old-Fashioned Community Centers: Region's country stores play important role," September 21, 1997, B8.

Dover Times, "Dover couple looks back at first year of owning Calef's," August 28, 1997, 6.

Heald, Bruce D. *Old Country Stores of New Hampshire*. Charleston, SC: The History Press. 2013. Heald writes about the lore, wares, and cachet of the country store. He includes most of the country stores still operating in New Hampshire, Calef's among them, and what makes each of them special.

The *Tri-Town Transcript* covered local news for Barrington and surrounding towns for decades. Though the *Transcript* has been gone for many years, Carolyn Handy, its last editor, saved the archives, all the old papers and photographs. A big thanks to her for helping us comb through many boxes to find photos and for letting us use them in this book.

Recipes from Calef's

Calef's Cheddar Cheese Crisps

Ingredients

- ½ cup unbleached all-purpose flour
- Salt, preferably sea or kosher
- Freshly ground black pepper
- 2 large egg whites, beaten
- ½ cup whole milk
- About 3 cups panko (coarse Japanese) or plain dry breadcrumbs
- ¼ cup ground almonds
- 12 (¼-inch-thick) crosswise slices from 8-ounce bar of Calef's Rat Trap Cheddar
- Vegetable oil
- Marinara sauce (optional)

Directions

1. In small bowl, combine flour with pinch of salt and pepper. In second small bowl, beat together egg whites and milk with fork or whisk until combined. In third bowl, stir together breadcrumbs and almonds.
2. Dip both sides of each cheese slice into flour, then egg white mixture, then breadcrumb mixture, making sure slice is completely covered. Place on large plate or baking sheet and place in freezer until firm, about 10 minutes. Discard any unused breadcrumb mixture.
3. Place large nonstick skillet over high heat and add enough oil to lightly cover bottom. When oil is hot, add frozen cheddar slices. Cook until golden brown on underside, then turn over and cook until golden on second side and melted inside. Serve with tomato sauce.

Cheesy Potato Croquettes

Ingredients

- 1 ½ pounds potatoes (about 5 medium potatoes), peeled
- ¼ cup water
- 8 ounces Calef's Rat Trap Cheddar, grated (about 2 cups)
- 1 teaspoon salt
- 1 teaspoon pepper
- ¼ cup Unbleached Whole Wheat Flour
- 2 large eggs, whisked
- 1 cup panko breadcrumbs
- Olive oil cooking spray
- Toppings: ketchup and parsley

Directions

1. Boil potatoes in water until tender, about 30–40 minutes depending on the size of the potatoes.
2. Preheat oven to 450°F.
3. Mash potatoes with a fork and add up to ¼ cup of water, if needed to make them stick together a bit more. Add the cheese, salt and pepper, and mix to incorporate completely.
4. Form the potato and cheese mixture into 12 croquettes (these will be large but you can also make them smaller). Coat each croquette in flour, dip into the egg mixture, and cover in breadcrumbs.
5. Place the croquettes on a baking sheet and generously spray each croquette with cooking spray. Bake for 15–20 minutes, or until lightly golden brown and cheese begins to bubble out.

Greek Yogurt Cheddar Biscuits

Ingredients

- o 2 cups all-purpose flour (plus more for the work surface)
- o 1 tablespoon baking powder
- o ½ teaspoon baking soda
- o 1 teaspoon kosher salt
- o ¾ cup plain Greek-style yogurt
- o 4 ounces cold Calef's Rat Trap Cheddar, shredded (about 1 cup)
- o ½ cup cold milk (or buttermilk)
- o 1 large cold egg

Egg Wash:

- o 1 egg + 1 tablespoon water

Directions

1. Preheat the oven to 400°F. Line a baking sheet with parchment paper or lightly spray with non-stick cooking spray.
2. In a large bowl whisk together the flour, baking powder, baking soda, and salt. Spoon the Greek yogurt into the bowl and add the cheese but don't combine the ingredients yet—put the bowl in the freezer.
3. Measure your buttermilk or milk into a liquid measuring cup and whisk in the egg. Put the mixture in the fridge for a minute while you mix up the egg wash and flour the counter where you'll be working.
4. Grab the bowl from the freezer and the milk/egg mix from the fridge. Pour the milk into the bowl and use a rubber spatula to combine everything. Add a little more flour if the dough seems too sticky.
5. Turn the dough out onto the prepared work surface and with floured hands pat it out to about ¾" thick. Cut 16 circles using a 2" biscuit cutter or a floured juice glass. If you are making "regular" biscuits you can just place the dough rounds on the prepared baking sheet, about 1½" apart. If you are making BIG FAT biscuits then you're going to stack the rounds you just cut out. There's no need to pinch the dough together or anything. Just stack two together and place them on the baking sheet about 2" apart.
6. Brush the tops of the biscuits with the egg wash and then bake for 12–14 minutes (for "regular" biscuits you can check them at 10 minutes).

Jalapeno Cornbread Crackers

Ingredients

- 1 cup whole-wheat white flour or unbleached all-purpose flour
- ½ cup cornmeal
- ¼ teaspoon baking powder
- ⅛ teaspoon salt
- ⅛ teaspoon smoked paprika
- 7 tablespoons slightly softened unsalted butter
- 5 ounces Calef's Buffalo Wing Cheddar, shredded (about 1 ¼ cups)
- ½ cup frozen corn, thawed and pureed
- 1 large egg, beaten

Directions

1. Line 2 baking sheets with parchment paper or spray lightly with cooking spray.
2. In bowl of stand mixer, mix together flour, cornmeal, baking powder, salt and smoked paprika. Cut butter into small pieces and toss with flour; sprinkle in cheese and mix. Turn on mixer and mix until dough looks sandy with a few pea-sized chunks; about 3–4 minutes. Add corn and egg; blend for 1 to 2 minutes longer until medium-firm dough is formed. Press dough into a ball, wrap in plastic wrap and chill in freezer for about 30 minutes.
3. Preheat oven to 375°F.
4. Unwrap dough and place on lightly floured work surface. Working with ¼th of the dough at a time, roll out into ⅛-inch-thick layer. With square or round or small animal-shaped cutters, cut out crackers and place on prepared baking sheets. Repeat with remaining dough. Bake crackers about 12–13 minutes or until barely light golden brown. Cool on baking rack.
5. Store in tightly covered container for up to one week.

Spicy Cheddar 'Cornbread' Muffins

Ingredients

- ½ cup coconut flour
- 2 tablespoons sugar
- ½ tablespoon baking powder
- ½ teaspoon kosher salt
- 2 teaspoons chili powder
- 3 large eggs, lightly beaten
- ½ cup milk
- ¼ cup canola oil
- 2 tablespoons cottage cheese
- 2 ounces Calef's Rat Trap Cheddar, grated (about ½ cup)
- 2 chopped green onions
- 1 to 2 canned chipotle peppers, chopped

Directions

1. Preheat oven to 325°F.
2. Coat 16 mini-muffin cups with cooking spray.
3. Whisk together coconut flour, sugar, baking powder, salt and chili powder in a medium-size bowl.
4. In a separate bowl, combine eggs, milk, oil and cottage cheese.
5. Add to dry ingredients and stir until well combined. Stir in cheese, green onion and chipotle peppers. Divide batter evenly among muffin cups. Baked at 325°F for 25 minutes (be careful not to burn).

Broccoli Cheddar Soup

Ingredients

- 2 tablespoons salted butter
- 2 cups peeled and diced boiling potatoes (about 2 medium)
- ½ cup chopped onion
- 2 tablespoons unbleached all-purpose flour
- 1 (14 ½-ounce) can chicken broth (about 2 cups)
- 2 cups milk
- 3 cups broccoli (chopped florets and thinly sliced stems)
- 8 ounces Calef's Rat Trap Cheddar, grated (about 2 cups)
- Pinch of lemon zest
- Salt and ground black pepper to taste

Directions

1. In large saucepan, melt butter over medium heat. Add potatoes and onion and cook, stirring, until onion is tender, about 5 minutes.
2. Add flour and cook, stirring, for 2 minutes longer.
3. Gradually stir in chicken broth and milk. Bring to simmer and cook until potatoes are nearly tender, about 5 minutes. Add broccoli and cook until broccoli is tender, about 5 minutes longer.
4. Remove from heat and stir in cheese. Add lemon zest and season with salt and pepper.

Onion Cheese Puffs

Grate 1 lb. Calef's Aged Cheddar.

Dice 1 small onion.

Mix cheese and onion with enough mayonnaise to be able to form walnut-sized balls.

Place balls on Triscuit® crackers.

Broil until they puff.

Cheddar Ale Soup

Ingredients

- O 4 slices bacon
- O 4 tablespoons salted butter
- O ½ cup minced onion
- O ¼ cup minced carrot
- O ¼ cup minced celery
- O 1 small bay leaf
- O ⅓ cup unbleached all-purpose flour
- O 1 (12-ounce) bottle ale
- O 2 ½ cups lowfat (1%) milk
- O 1 (14-ounce) can 99% fat-free chicken broth
- O 1 teaspoon dry mustard
- O 1 pound Calef's Rat Trap Cheddar, grated (about 4 cups)
- O Salt and ground black pepper to taste.

Directions

1. In skillet or microwave, cook bacon until crisp; crumble and set aside.
2. In large saucepan over medium heat, melt butter; add onion, carrot, celery and bay leaf and cook, stirring often, until vegetables are translucent and softened, about 4 minutes.
3. Stir in flour and cook, stirring, about 3 minutes longer.
4. Gradually whisk in ale; stirring for about two minutes or until mixture is bubbling and thickened. Whisk in milk, chicken broth and dry mustard. Bring soup to simmer, stirring often so it doesn't scorch on bottom of pan.
5. Add cheese a handful at a time; stir until cheese is melted and soup is hot, but do not let soup boil. Remove from heat, remove and discard bay leaf and season with salt and pepper.
6. Serve topped with crumbled bacon.

Savory Bread Pudding

Ingredients

- 6 large eggs
- 1 cup lowfat (1%) milk
- ½ teaspoon salt
- ¼ teaspoon ground black pepper
- Dried or fresh herbs to taste
- 3 cups cubed bread (leftover dinner rolls or extra bread from stuffing)
- 3 cups diced mixed cooked vegetables (such as onions, bell peppers, zucchini, spinach, fennel, broccoli, mushrooms, tomatoes, carrots
- 8 ounces Calef's Rat Trap Cheddar, grated and divided, (about 2 cups)

Directions

1. Preheat oven to 350°F. Grease 7-by-11-inch baking dish.
2. In large bowl, whisk together eggs, milk and seasonings. Fold in cubed bread, vegetables and 1 ½ cups of cheese.
3. Pour into baking dish and sprinkle with remaining ½ cup cheese.
4. Bake for 35 to 45 minutes or until set all the way to center.

Cuban Bite

Ingredients

- Calef's Rat Trap Cheddar
- Pretzel Crisps® (your choice of flavor)
- Ham (cooked)
- Pickle (chips or sliced)
- Yellow mustard

Directions

Add a slice of cheese, a piece of cooked ham, yellow mustard and a pickle between your favorite flavor of Pretzel Crisps®.

Apple Pie & Cheddar Pretzel Crisps

Ingredients

- 1 unpeeled apple, such as Cortland, Fuji or Granny Smith, quartered, cored and very thinly sliced
- 2 teaspoons butter
- 1 tablespoon sugar
- About 2 dozen Cinnamon Toast Pretzel Crisps
- 4 ounces Calef's Rat Trap Cheddar, thinly sliced
- Ground cinnamon

Directions

1. In large skillet, melt butter over medium heat. Add apples and cook, stirring often, until apples begin to soften and brown, about 5 minutes.
2. Add sugar and continue stirring for about 5 more minutes until apples are tender and lightly browned.
3. Top each pretzel crisp with cheddar and slices of apple. Sprinkle with additional cinnamon if desired.

Basic Cheddar Cheese Sauce

Ingredients

- 8 tablespoons (1 stick) salted butter
- ½ cup unbleached all-purpose flour
- 4 cups hot milk (1%)
- 16 ounces Calef's Rat Trap Cheddar, grated (about 4 cups)

Directions

1. Melt butter in large heavy-bottomed saucepan over medium heat. Whisk in flour a little at a time until well blended. Continue stirring for a minute or two longer.
2. Gradually whisk in milk and continue stirring until sauce is thickened. Add cheese, stirring until melted and blended.

Apple, Cranberry & Cheddar Muffins

Ingredients

- 2 cups unbleached all-purpose flour
- ⅓ cup sugar
- 3 teaspoons baking powder
- ½ teaspoon salt
- 4 ounces Calef's Rat Trap Cheddar, grated (about 1 cup)
- ¾ cup Ocean Spray Cranberry Juice Cocktail
- ⅓ cup canola or other vegetable oil
- 1 large egg
- 1 cup peeled and finely diced apples
- ½ cup Ocean Spray Craisins Original Dried Cranberries

Directions

1. Preheat oven to 400°F. Coat insides of 12-hole muffin pan with cooking spray or line with muffin cups.
2. In mixing bowl, whisk together flour, sugar, baking powder and salt. Stir in grated cheddar.
3. In another bowl, whisk together cranberry juice, vegetable oil and egg. Add juice mixture to dry ingredients along with apples and cranberries; stir just until dry ingredients are incorporated, but batter is still lumpy.
4. Fill muffin cups about two-thirds full. Bake for 15 to 20 minutes or until nicely browned on top and skewer inserted in center comes out clean. Let stand for about 1 minute before removing from pan.

Breakfast Sausage Bake

Ingredients

- O Nonstick cooking spray
- O 4 slices whole-grain or white bread
- O 1 pound bulk sausage, browned and drained
- O 6 large eggs
- O 2 cups milk
- O 1 tablespoon yellow mustard
- O ½ teaspoon salt
- O ¼ teaspoon ground black pepper
- O 4 ounces Calef's Rat Trap Cheddar, grated (about 1 cup)

Directions

1. Preheat oven to 350°F. Coat 8-by-10-inch or similar-sized baking dish with nonstick cooking spray.
2. Tear bread into small pieces and scatter over bottom of dish. Top with sausage.
3. In medium bowl, whisk eggs until combined; whisk in milk, mustard, salt and pepper. Pour over bread and sausage. Sprinkle cheese over top.
4. Bake uncovered for 35 to 45 minutes or until set all the way to center (knife inserted in center comes out clean).

Caramelized Onion Melts

Ingredients

- ○ Sea Salt & Cracked Pepper Pretzel Crisps®
- ○ Calef's Rat Trap Cheddar Cheese
- ○ Caramelized Onions

Directions

Stack caramelized onions and a slice of Calef's Cheddar cheese on top of Sea Salt & Cracked Pepper Pretzel Crisps®. Heat the cheese into melty goodness and then serve!

Smoky Cheese Chowder Recipe

Ingredients

- ○ 1 10-oz. pkg. frozen whole kernel corn
- ○ ½ cup chopped onion
- ○ ½ cup water
- ○ 1 tsp. instant chicken bouillon granules
- ○ ¼ tsp. pepper
- ○ 2 ½ cups milk
- ○ 3 Tbsp. all-purpose flour
- ○ 4 oz. grated Calef's Smoked Cheddar
- ○ 1 Tbsp. diced pimento, drained

Directions

In a saucepan combine corn, onion, water, bouillon, & pepper. Bring to a boil, reduce heat. Cover & simmer about 4 minutes or until corn is tender. Do not drain. Stir together milk & flour; then stir into corn mixture until thickened & bubbly. Stir in pimento & cheese until cheese melts & serve hot. Serves four.

Cheese Coins

Cream 2 cups (about ½ pound) grated Calef's Aged Cheddar with ½ cup margarine or butter. Add 1 and ½ cups flour.

Mix in your choice of one of the following: 1 Tablespoon chives, ½ teaspoon onion powder, ½ teaspoon cayenne pepper, or ½ teaspoon Tabasco sauce.

Roll dough into a 2-inch diameter log, wrap in cellophane or wax paper and refrigerate for at least 2 hours. You may also freeze these logs for baking at a later date.

After refrigeration, slice very thin (like coins) and bake on an ungreased cookie sheet at 350°F for 15 minutes or until lightly browned.

Cheese Balls

Cream 1 cup (about ¼ pound) of grated Calef's Aged Cheddar with ½ cup butter or margarine.

Mix in 1 cup flour, ½ teaspoon Tabasco sauce, and 1 cup of Rice Krispies©.

Shape into marble-sized balls and ungreased baking sheet at 350°F for 10–12 minutes or until lightly browned.

Store the Cheese Balls in a closed container in your refrigerator.

Spinach & Cheddar Squares

Ingredients

- ○ 3 eggs
- ○ 1 cup flour
- ○ 1 cup milk
- ○ 1 teaspoon salt
- ○ 1 teaspoon baking powder
- ○ 2 packages thawed spinach
- ○ 1 Tablespoon chopped onion
- ○ 4 Tablespoons margarine
- ○ 1 pound shredded Calef's Aged Cheddar

Directions

Mix together eggs, flour, milk, salt, and baking powder.

Once well mixed, add Cheddar, spinach, and onion.

Use the margarine to grease well a 9x13 pan and then add the remaining margarine to the mixture.

Pour the mixture into pan and bake at 350°F for 35 minutes.

Cut the mixture into squares for warm canapés or larger pieces for a lunch. You may freeze the Spinach Squares for reheating later.

Mary Calef Cheese Soup

Ingredients

- 6 ounces Calef's Aged Cheddar grated
- 6 ounces Rat Trap Cheddar grated
- 4 Tablespoons butter
- ½ cup diced carrot
- ½ cup diced green pepper
- ½ cup minced onion
- ½ cup minced celery
- ½ cup flour
- 1 quart well-seasoned chicken stock
- 3–4 cups fresh milk
- salt and white pepper

Directions

1. Melt butter in double boiler, add vegetables.
2. Braise vegetables until tender, not brown.
3. Blend in flour. Cook one minute, stirring constantly.
4. Add stock and cook; stir until thick.
5. Add Cheddars; stir until they melt.
6. Thin with milk to creamy consistency.
7. Season with salt & pepper.
8. Strain, Reheat in double boiler.
9. Serve hot—or in warm weather, serve very cold.

Cheddar Pumpkin Dip

Ingredients

- Non-stick cooking spray
- 1 can cannellini beans, drained and rinsed
- 1 ½ cups pumpkin puree (fresh pumpkin roasted is tastier, canned is easier)
- 1 clove garlic, minced
- Salt and pepper, to taste
- 6 ounces Calef's Buffalo Wing Cheddar, shredded (about 1 ½ cups)
- Sundried tomatoes, roma tomatoes and/or green onions, for garnish
- Tortilla chips, carrot sticks and celery sticks, for dipping

Directions

1. Preheat oven to 350°F. Spray six ramekins with non-stick cooking spray.
2. Combine cannellini beans, pumpkin, garlic, salt and pepper in food processor and puree until smooth.
3. Divide mixture between the six ramekins. Sprinkle the cheese on top of the bean and pumpkin mixture and stir to incorporate the cheese throughout. Sprinkle top with diced sundried tomatoes, if using.
4. Bake for 15 minutes or until bubbling and heated throughout.
5. Garnish with tomatoes and/or green onion, if using. Serve with chips and veggies to dip.

Cheesy Cheddar Stuffed Meatballs

Ingredients

Meatballs:

- 1 ¼ pounds ground beef
- ½ onion, finely chopped
- 1 inch piece of ginger, finely chopped
- 2 cloves garlic, finely chopped
- ¼ teaspoon salt
- ½ teaspoon pepper
- 1 teaspoon turmeric
- 1 teaspoon paprika
- 2 teaspoons chopped cilantro
- 2 ounces Calef's Rat Trap Cheddar, grated (about ½ cup)
- 1 egg
- Calef's Aged Cheddar, cut into cubes

Spicy Cheese Dipping Sauce:

- ½ cup milk
- 3 ounces Calef's Rat Trap Cheddar, grated (about ¾ cup)
- ¼ teaspoon chili powder
- ¼ teaspoon paprika

Directions

Meatballs:

1. Preheat oven to 375°F.
2. Mix all the ingredients together, except for the cubed cheddar.
3. Mix into a ball, enclosing a cube of cheddar in the middle.
4. Bake at 375°F for 30 minutes.

Spicy Cheese Dipping Sauce:

1. Place milk, cheese, chili powder and paprika in a saucepan over medium heat for about 10 minutes. Stir frequently so cheese melts evenly.
2. Serve with meatballs.

About the Author

Rebecca Rule is a full-time writer, humorist, storyteller, host for ten years of the NH Authors Series on NHPTV, and currently host of Our Hometown on NHPTV. She's been telling stories in New England, especially New Hampshire, for more than twenty years. She hasn't visited every town in the Granite State, but pretty close—speaking at libraries, historical societies, rotaries, clubs, church groups, camp grounds, and charitable organizations. Some of her talks are sponsored by NH Humanities, which named her one of 40 Over 40, that is, one of forty New Hampshire folks who over the past forty years of the Council's existence "have demonstrated what it means to create, teach, lead, assist, and encourage human understanding."

She's the author of eleven books including *N is for NH*, an ABC book with photographs by Scott Snyder. Other books include *The Iciest Diciest Scariest Sled Ride Ever!*, a picture book, illustrated by Jennifer Thermes; *Moved and Seconded: NH Town Meeting*; *Headin' for the Rhubarb, A NH Dictionary (well, kinda)*; and *The Best Revenge*, named one of five essential NH Books by "NH Magazine" and Outstanding Work of Fiction by the NH Writers Project.

Her children's books take her into schools. Her humor takes her to senior centers and assisted living facilities.

She lives in Northwood with her husband, John Rule, six cats and three dogs, all rescues—except for John Rule and Reggie, a wire fox terrier. She loves cheese.